Contents

Chapter Five   69

TOPICS
Morning routines
Locations
Leisure activities
Colors
Clothes

GRAMMAR
Present continuous
Wh- questions

FUNCTIONS
Describing actions
Describing people's dress
Talking on the telephone

Chapter Six   84

TOPICS
Physical characteristics
Small talk

GRAMMAR
"To have"
Possessive adjectives
Possessive of nouns
"Whose . . . ?"

FUNCTIONS
Identifying possessions
Describing people
Getting and giving personal information

Chapter Seven   101

TOPICS
Food and drinks
The home and furniture

GRAMMAR
There is/there are
Some/any
Countables and uncountables
"To like," "to want," "to need"

FUNCTIONS
Asking about quantity
Expressing preferences in food
Expressing satisfaction/dissatisfaction
Expressing likes/dislikes
Expressing want/desire
Expressing need

Chapter Eight   119

TOPICS
Art exhibition
Popular entertainment
A trip to Paris
Leisure activities

GRAMMAR
Review

FUNCTIONS
Expressing preferences in entertainment
Indicating location
Describing actions
Making suggestions
Offering to help
Expressing need
Apologizing
Expressing disappointment
Expressing gratitude

Preview   136

GRAMMAR
Can
Simple past
Future with "going to"

FUNCTIONS
Expressing ability/inability
Describing past actions
Expressing intention

Appendix   141

Irregular verbs
Pronunciation
Vocabulary

Preface

Exploring English is a comprehensive, six-level course for adult and young adult students of English. It teaches all four language skills—listening, speaking, reading, and writing—with an emphasis on oral communication. The course combines a strong grammar base with in-depth coverage of language functions and life skills.

Exploring English:

Teaches grammar inductively. The basic structures are introduced in context through illustrated situations and dialogues. Students use the structures in talking about the situations and re-enacting the dialogues. They encounter each structure in a variety of contexts, including practice exercises, pair work activities, and readings. This repeated exposure enables students to make reliable and useful generalizations about the language. They develop a "language sense"—a feeling for words—that carries over into their daily use of English.

Includes language functions in every chapter from beginning through advanced levels. Guided conversations, discussions, and role plays provide varied opportunities to practice asking for and giving information, expressing likes and dislikes, agreeing and disagreeing, and so on.

Develops life skills in the areas most important to students: food, clothing, transportation, work, housing, and health care. Everyday life situations provide contexts for learning basic competencies: asking directions, taking a bus, buying food, shopping for clothes, and so on. Students progress from simpler tasks, such as describing occupations at the beginning level, to interviewing for jobs and discussing problems at work at more advanced levels.

Incorporates problem solving and critical thinking in many of the lessons, especially at the intermediate and advanced levels. The stories in *Exploring English* present a cast of colorful characters who get involved in all kinds of life problems, ranging from personal relationships to work-related issues to politics. Students develop critical-thinking skills as they discuss these problems, give their opinions, and try to find solutions. These discussions also provide many opportunities for students to talk about their own lives.

Provides extensive practice in listening comprehension through illustrated situations. Students are asked to describe each illustration in their own words before listening to the accompanying story (which appears on the reverse side of the page). Then they answer questions based on the story, while looking at the illustration. The students respond to what they see and hear without referring to text, just as in actual conversation.

Offers students frequent opportunities for personal expression. The emphasis throughout *Exploring English* is on communication—encouraging students to use the language to express their own ideas and feelings. Free response questions in Books 1 and 2 give students the opportunity to talk about themselves using simple, straightforward English. Every chapter in Books 3–6 has a special section, called "One Step Further," that includes discussion topics such as work, leisure activities, cinema, travel, dating, and marriage. Ideas for role plays are also provided to give additional opportunities for free expression. The general themes are familiar to students because they draw on material already covered in the same chapter. Role plays give students a chance to interact spontaneously—perhaps the most important level of practice in developing communication skills.

Provides continuous review and reinforcement. Each chapter concludes with a review section and every fourth chapter is devoted entirely to review, allowing students to practice newly acquired language in different combinations.

Provides exposure to key structures that students will be learning at the next level. This material, included in a special unit called "Preview," can be introduced at any time during the course at the discretion of the teacher.

Presents attractive art that visually supports and is integral with the language being taught. Humorous and imaginative illustrations, in full color, make *Exploring English* fun for students. In addition, the richness of the art allows teachers to devise their own spin-off activities, increasing the teachability of each page.

Each volume of *Exploring English* is accompanied by a Workbook. The Workbook lessons are closely coordinated to the lessons in the Student Book. They provide additional writing practice using the same grammatical structures and vocabulary while expanding on basic functions and life skills. The activities range from sentence completion exercises to guided paragraph and composition writing.

Student Books and Workbooks include clear labels and directions for each activity. In addition, Teacher's Resource Manuals are available for each level. These Manuals provide step-by-step guidance for teaching each page, expansion activities, and answers to the exercises. Each student page is reproduced for easy reference.

Audiocassettes for each level featuring an entertaining variety of native voices round out the series. All of the dialogues, readings, and pronunciation exercises are included on the tapes.

Chapter

1

Listen and practice.

PETER: Hello. What's your name?

MARIA: My name's Maria.

PETER: My name's Peter.

MARIA: Nice to meet you, Peter.

PAIR WORK 1 • *Have similar conversations.*

STUDENT A: Hello. What's your name?

STUDENT B: My name's _____.

STUDENT A: My name's _____.

STUDENT B: Nice to meet you, _____.

 Listen and practice.

BARBARA: Good morning.

TINO: Good morning. How are you?

BARBARA: I'm fine. And you?

TINO: Fine, thank you.

PAIR WORK 2 • *Have similar conversations.*

Listen and practice.

GROUP WORK • *Have similar conversations.*

STUDENT A: _____, this is _____.

STUDENT B: Nice to meet you, _____.

STUDENT C: Nice to meet you, too.

Listen and practice.

PAIR WORK • *Have similar conversations.*

STUDENT A: Good-bye, _____.

STUDENT B: Bye. See you later.

Listen and repeat.

This is John Bascomb.

He's a banker.

This is Maria Miranda.

She's a doctor.

This is Peter Smith.

He's a businessman.

This is Anne Jones.

She's a secretary.

This is Nancy Paine.

She isn't a doctor.

She's a pilot.

This is Otis Jackson.

He isn't a businessman.

He's an artist.

This is Ula Hackey.

She isn't a secretary.

She's a movie star.

This is Nick Vitakis.

He isn't a banker.

He's a mechanic.

Listen and practice.

FRED: Who's that?

BARNEY: Her name is Nancy Paine.

FRED: Is she a mechanic?

BARNEY: No, she isn't. She's a pilot.

FRED: What's his name?

BARNEY: Otis Jackson.

FRED: Is he a pilot, too?

BARNEY: No, he isn't. He's an artist.

Listen and practice.

1. What's this?   It's a book.

2. What's this?   It's a chair.

3. What's this?   _____ bottle.

4. What's this?   _____ hat.

5. Is this a clock?   Yes, it is.

6. Is this a table?   Yes, it is.

7. Is this a book?   No, it isn't.
   What is it?   It's a newspaper.

8. Is this a bottle?   No, it isn't.
   What is it?   _____ glass.

9. Is this a clock?   _____.
   What is it?   _____ watch.

10. Is this a hat?   _____.
    What is it?   _____ coat.

Listen and practice.

1. What's this?
   It's a rabbit.

2. What's this?
   It's a chicken.

3. What's _____?
   It's a pear.

4. What's that?   It's a bird.

5. What's that?   It's a dog.

6. What's _____?   _____ an apple.

7. Is that a cat?   Yes, it is.

8. Is this a dog?
   No, it isn't.

   It's a _____.

9. Is _____ an apple?
   No, it isn't.

   It's a _____.

10. Is _____ an apple?   Yes, it is.

Listen and practice.

1. What are these?
   They're flowers.

2. What are these?
   They're cards.

3. What are _____?
   They're rabbits.

4. What are those?   They're chickens.

5. What are those?   They're cats.

6. What are _____?   _____ dogs.

7. Are these rabbits? Yes, they are.

8. Are those pears?   Yes, they are.

9. Are _____ cats?
   No, they aren't.
   They're _____.

10. Are _____ apples?
    No, they aren't. They're _____.

🔊 *Listen and repeat.*

The cat is <u>under</u> the table.

The ball is <u>in front of</u> the cat.

The vase is <u>on</u> the table.

The flower is <u>in</u> the vase.

The envelope is <u>on</u> the table.

The envelope is <u>next to</u> the vase.

The bookcase is <u>behind</u> the table.

The books are <u>in</u> the bookcase.

PAIR WORK • *Ask and answer questions. Choose the correct preposition.*

Student A: **Where's the cat now?**
Student B: **It's on the table.**

1. Where's the dog?
   It's (on/under) the table.

2. Where's the vase?
   It's (on/under) the floor.

3. Where's the flower?
   It's (in/next to) the vase.

4. Where's the envelope?
   It's (in front of/behind) the cat.

5. Where's the ball?
   It's (in front of/behind) the dog.

WRITTEN EXERCISE • *Complete the sentences using these prepositions: **in, on, under, next to, behind,** and **in front of.***

Simon is ___*behind*___ the door.

1. The rabbit is _____ the hat.

2. The chicken is _____ the table.

3. The apples are _____ the table.

4. The flowers are _____ the vase.

5. The bottle is _____ the vase.

6. Suzi is _____ the clock.

7. The dog is _____ the clock.

8. The clock is _____ the bookcase.

9. The books are _____ the bookcase.

10. The cat is _____ the newspaper.

11. The ball is _____ the cat.

12. The coat is _____ the chair.

PAIR WORK • *Ask and answer questions.*

	apples		dog
Student A:	**Where are the apples?**	Student A:	**Where is the dog?**
Student B:	**They're on the table.**	Student B:	**It's in front of the clock.**

1. books
2. Suzi
3. coat
4. ball
5. chicken
6. flowers
7. bottle
8. Simon
9. rabbit

Listen and repeat.

1.

Ula Hackey is at the movies.

2.

Otis is at the museum.

3.

Mr. Bascomb is at the bank.

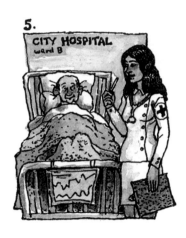

4.

Nick is at the garage.

5.

Maria is at the hospital.

6.

Peter is at the office.

7.

Nancy is at the airport.

8.

Anne is at the post office.

9.

Barney is at the gas station.

PRACTICE • *Look at the pictures on page 12. Replace with **he** or **she**.*

1. Ula is at the movies.
   She's at the movies.
2. Otis is at the museum.
   He's at the museum.
3. Mr. Bascomb is at the bank.
4. Nick is at the garage.

5. Maria is at the hospital.
6. Peter is at the office.
7. Nancy is at the airport.
8. Anne is at the post office.
9. Barney is at the gas station.

PAIR WORK • *Look at the pictures on page 12. Ask and answer questions.*

1. A. **Is Ula at the movies?**
   B. **Yes, she is.**
2. A. **Is Otis at the post office?**
   B. **No, he isn't. He's at the museum.**
3. Is Mr. Bascomb at the hospital?
4. Is Nick at the garage?

5. Is Maria at the airport?
6. Is Peter at the office?
7. Is Nancy at the movies?
8. Is Anne at the bank?
9. Is Barney at the gas station?

WRITTEN EXERCISE • *Complete with **a** or **an**.*

It's __*a*__ glass.   It's __*an*__ egg.

1. It's _____ tree.
2. It's _____ apple.
3. It's _____ car.

4. It's _____ bottle.
5. It's _____ orange.
6. It's _____ envelope.

7. It's _____ library.
8. It's _____ newspaper.
9. It's _____ airport.

a car

a library

a tree

an apple   an orange   an egg

Note: **a** before consonant   **an** before a, e, i, o, u

WRITTEN EXERCISE • *Look at the picture and complete the sentences. Use* ***at, in, on, under, next to, in front of,*** *and* ***behind.***

> Where's the bus stop? It's _____*at*_____ the corner.

1. Where's Barbara? She's _____ the bus stop.

2. Where's the truck? It's _____ the bus.

3. Where's the post office? It's _____ the garage.

4. Where's the tree? It's _____ the garage.

5. Where's the car? It's _____ the garage.

6. Where's Nick? He's _____ the car.

PAIR WORK • *Ask and answer questions about the picture.*

> Student A: Is the bus stop at the corner?
> Student B: **Yes, It is.**
>
> Student A: Is Barbara in the post office?
> Student B: **No, she isn't. She's at the bus stop.**

1. Is the truck behind the bus?
2. Is the post office next to the garage?
3. Is the tree behind the post office?
4. Is the car in front of the garage?
5. Is Nick in the car?

WRITTEN EXERCISE • *Complete the sentences.*

1. What's _*this*_ ? It's _*a hat*_ .

2. What's _____ ? It's _____ .

3. What's _____ ? It's _____ .

4. What's _____ ? It's _____ .

5. What are _____ ? They're _____ .

6. What are _____ ? They're _____ .

7. What are _____ ? They're _____ .

8. What are _____ ? They're _____ .

1. Tony Romero/singer

2. Susan Steel/police officer

3. Donald Poole/teacher

A: **Who's that?**	A: **Who's that?**
B: **His name is Tony Romero.**	B: **Her name is Susan Steel.**
A: **What's his job?**	A: **What's her job?**
B: **He's a singer.**	B: **She's a police officer.**

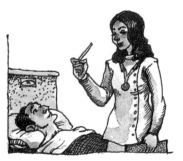

4. Maria Miranda/doctor

5. Nick Vitakis/mechanic

6. Nancy Paine/pilot

7. Otis Jackson/artist

8. Florence Golo/teacher

9. John Bascomb/banker

10. Anne Jones/secretary

11. Peter Smith/businessman

12. Bonita Cantata/singer

GRAMMAR SUMMARY

TO BE Affirmative

He She It	's (is)	in the office.

Negative

He She It	isn't (is not) 's not	in the office.

Interrogative

Is	he she it	in the office?

Short Answers

Yes,	he she it	is.	No,	he she it	isn't.

Question with WHAT

What	's (is)	this? that?
	are	these? those?

SINGULAR AND PLURAL NOUNS

It	's (is)	a pear. an apple.
They	're (are)	cards. flowers.

Question with WHERE

Where	's (is)	Mr. Bascomb?
	's (is)	the newspaper?
	are	the books?

PREPOSITIONS

He	's (is)	at in	the bank. his office.
It	's (is)	on under next to behind in front of	the table.
They	're (are)		

Question with WHO

Who	's (is)	that?	Otis Jackson.

Chapter 2

TOPICS
Colors
Clothes
Numbers 1–20
Time

GRAMMAR
"To be" (continued)
Adjectives
Singular and plural nouns

FUNCTIONS
Asking where others are from
Describing people
Giving compliments
Asking for and telling the time

Listen and repeat.

CONVERSATION

 Listen and practice.

WAITER: Excuse me. Are you a tourist?

TOURIST: Yes, I am.

WAITER: Are you English?

TOURIST: No, I'm not.

WAITER: What nationality are you?

TOURIST: I'm American.

PAIR WORK • *Ask and answer questions.*

A: Are you an artist?
B: **Yes, I am.** OR **No, I'm not.**

1. Are you Italian?
2. Are you a student?
3. Are you rich?
4. Are you married?
5. Are you a tourist?
6. Are you hot?
7. Are you thirsty?
8. Are you happy?
9. Are you sad?
10. Are you cold?

happy   sad

CONVERSATIONS

PEDRO: Are you from the United States?

STEVE: Yes, we are. We're from Hollywood.

PEDRO: Are you movie stars?

STEVE: No, we aren't movie stars. We're students.

JUANITA: Who are they?

PEDRO: They're Americans. They're from Hollywood.

JUANITA: Are they movie stars?

PEDRO: No, they aren't. They're students.

PRACTICE

1. Replace with **you**, **we**, *or* **they**.

Barney and I are friends.
We're friends.

1. <u>Anne and Nancy</u> are Americans.
2. <u>You and Nancy</u> are from New York.
3. <u>Anne and Peter</u> are from Los Angeles.
4. <u>Anne and I</u> are friends.
5. <u>You and Nancy</u> are friends.
6. <u>You and I</u> are students.
7. <u>Those girls</u> are students.

2. Change the sentences to questions.

They're bankers.
Are they bankers?

1. They're at a meeting.
2. They're at the City Bank.
3. They're on Franklin Avenue.
4. We're on Main Street.
5. We're at the post office.
6. You're doctors.
7. You're from the hospital.

3. Change the sentences to the negative.

You're movie stars.
You aren't movie stars.

1. You're tourists.
2. You're from England.
3. You're rich.
4. We're happy.
5. We're teachers.
6. They're pilots.
7. They're Americans.

Listen to the stories and answer the questions.

1 Tino is a waiter. He's tall and handsome. He isn't rich, but he's happy. Barbara is a secretary. She's short and blond. And she's beautiful. Barbara and Tino are good friends. They're from California.

   1. Is Tino a businessman?
   2. Is he short?
   3. Is he handsome?
   4. Is he rich?
   5. Is Barbara a secretary?
   6. Is she tall?
   7. Is she blond?
   8. Is she beautiful?
   9. Are Barbara and Tino good friends?
 10. Are they from New York?

2 Natalya and Boris are Russian ballet dancers. They're from Moscow. They're very good dancers.

   1. Are Natalya and Boris ballet dancers or movie stars?
   2. Where are they from?
   3. Are they good dancers?

3 Sammy and Tammy are country singers. They're from Nashville. They aren't very good singers. In fact, they're very bad.

   1. Are Sammy and Tammy singers or dancers?
   2. Where are they from?
   3. Are they good singers?

Listen and repeat.

This woman is fat.

That man is thin.

This bicycle is cheap.

That bicycle is expensive.

These women are young.

Those men are old.

These boys are dirty.

Those girls are clean.

WRITTEN EXERCISE • *Complete the sentences using "to be" and these adjectives:* ***bad, clean, beautiful, hot, cheap, fat, rich, married, short.***

1. Barbara *is beautiful*.

2. Mr. and Mrs. Bascomb _____.

3. Mr. Twaddle _____.

4. Mrs. Brown _____.

5. Albert _____.

6. Tino _____.

7. The pots _____.

8. The guitar _____.

9. The apples _____.

PAIR WORK • *Ask and answer questions.*

1. A: Is Barbara beautiful?
   B: **Yes, she is.**
2. A: Are Mr. and Mrs. Bascomb poor?
   B: **No, they aren't. They're rich.**
3. Is Mr. Twaddle tall?
4. Is Mrs. Brown married?

5. Is Albert thin?
6. Is Tino cold?
7. Are the pots clean?
8. Is the guitar expensive?
9. Are the apples good?

NEW VOCABULARY • COLORS AND CLOTHES

 Listen and repeat.

red   orange   yellow   green   blue   white   black   gray   brown

shirt   pants   dress   blouse   sweater   shoes

PRACTICE 1

What colors are the clothes above?

The shirt is red. The pants are blue.

PRACTICE 2

What color are your clothes?

My shirt is green. My shoes are black.

CONVERSATION

 Listen and practice.

TINO: That's a beautiful dress, Barbara.

BARBARA: Thank you, Tino.

TINO: Red is a good color for you.

BARBARA: Yes. It's my favorite color.

PAIR WORK • *Have similar conversations. Use new vocabulary such as **shirt, dress,** and **sweater.***

A: That's a beautiful shirt, _____.

B: Thank you, _____.

A: _____ is a good color for you.

B: Yes. It's my favorite color.

Listen and repeat.

one two three four five six seven eight nine ten

eleven twelve thirteen fourteen fifteen sixteen seventeen eighteen nineteen twenty

1 2 3 4 5 6 7 8 9 10 11 12 13 14 15 16 17 18 19 20

Listen and practice.

What time is it?
It's one o'clock.

What time is it?
It's eight o'clock.

What time is it?
It's three o'clock.

PAIR WORK • *Ask and answer questions.*

1.

2.

3.

A: **What time is it?**
B: **It's six o'clock.**

4.

5.

6.

7.

8.

9.

Listen and practice.

ALBERT: Who's that girl over there?

MR. WATKINS: Her name's Lúcia Mendes.

ALBERT: She's very pretty. Is she a student?

MR. WATKINS: Yes. She's a history student.

ALBERT: Is Lúcia Mexican?

MR. WATKINS: No, she isn't. She's Brazilian.

ALBERT: What city is she from?

MR. WATKINS: She's from Rio de Janeiro.

ALBERT: Is that the capital of Brazil?

MR. WATKINS: No. Brasília is the capital.

ALBERT: What's Brasília like?

MR. WATKINS: It's a beautiful modern city.

DIALOGUE QUESTIONS

1. Who's Albert with?
2. Is Mr. Watkins an intelligent man?
3. Who's the girl by the window?
4. Is she very pretty?
5. Is she American?
6. What nationality is she?
7. What city is she from?
8. Is Rio de Janeiro the capital of Brazil?
9. What is the capital of Brazil?
10. What's Brasília like?
11. What's the capital of your country?
12. What's your capital like?

PAIR WORK • *Ask and answer questions about the students in your class.*

A: Who's that student over there?

B: His/her name is _____.

A: Is he/she Mexican? /Chinese? /French?

B: _____.

A: What city is he/she from?

B: _____.

WRITTEN EXERCISE • *Put a or an before each word.*

1. *a* postcard   2. *an* umbrella   3. ____ wastebasket   4. ____ eye

5. ____ letter   6. ____ dictionary   7. ____ airplane   8. ____ magazine

1. How much is this dress?
   Fifty dollars.

2. ?
   I'm a mechanic.

3. ?
   I'm from Saudi Arabia.

4. ?
   My name's Marianne.

5. ?
   I'm fine.

6. ?
   That's my girlfriend.

7. ?
   It's a computer.

8. ?
   Under the table.

9. ?
   It's two o'clock.

GROUP WORK • *Have similar conversations with two other students in your class.*

Listen and repeat.

tall≠short	strong≠weak	hot≠cold	rich≠poor
fat≠thin	clean≠dirty	black≠white	beautiful≠ugly
old≠young	big≠small	happy≠sad	cheap≠expensive

PRACTICE • *Describe the people and objects in the pictures. Use the adjectives in the box.*

1. Tino   Johnnie

Tino is strong.
Johnnie is weak.

2. Barbara   Bernice

Barbara is beautiful.
Bernice is ugly.

3. apple   pear

The apple is big.
The pear is small.

4. Mr. Bascomb   Eddie

5. umbrella   hat

6. Mrs. Morley   Linda

7. guitar   violin

8. Mr. Poole   Mrs. Poole

9. Suzl   Nobu

10. coffee   lemonade

11. Jenny   Marty

12. Lotta   Bill

STRESS

doctor   expensive   behind

student   intelligent   garage

hospital   American   police

favorite   museum   hotel

telephone   umbrella   today

dangerous   mechanic   tonight

INTONATION

Where's Anne?   Are you hungry?   Is Tony a singer or a dancer?

She's at work.   Yes, I am.   He's a singer.

STRESS AND INTONATION

Excuse me. Are you a tourist?   Is John a doctor?

Yes, I am.   No, he isn't. He's a banker.

Are you English?   What city is he from?

No, I'm not.   He's from Wickam City.

What nationality are you?

I'm American.

Is your name Barney or Fred?

My name is Barney.

GRAMMAR SUMMARY

TO BE Affirmative

He She It	's (is)	
I	'm (am)	in the library.
You We They	're (are)	

Negative

He She It	isn't (is not) 's not	
I	'm not (am not)	in the library.
You We They	aren't (are not) 're not	

Interrogative

Is	he she it	
Am	I	in the library?
Are	you we they	

Short Answers

Yes,	he she it	is.	No,	he she it	isn't.
	I	am.		I	'm not.
	you we they	are.		you we they	aren't.

ADJECTIVES AND WORD ORDER

The city The buildings	is are	beautiful. modern.	It's They're	a beautiful city. modern buildings.

PREPOSITIONS

Albert is Lúcia is She's	with from by	Mr. Watkins. Rio de Janeiro. the window.

PLURALS

bus	buses	city	cities
watch	watches	library	libraries
glass	glasses	secretary	secretaries

Irregular

man	men
woman	women
child	children

Chapter

TOPICS
Numbers and time (continued)
Furniture
Emergencies
Locations

GRAMMAR
Imperative
Object pronouns

FUNCTIONS
Giving and understanding commands
Asking for and telling the time
Reporting an emergency
Inquiring about location
Asking about prices

Listen and repeat.

Close your book.

Stand up.

Go to the blackboard.

Write your name.

Sit down.

Be quiet.

Don't talk.

Don't write on the table.

Don't open the window.

Don't eat in class.

Don't leave the room.

Don't laugh.

Listen and repeat.

Hello, Johnnie. Come with <u>me</u>.

Oh, this bottle! Please open <u>it</u>.

There's Barbara and Tino.
Let's talk with <u>them</u>.

Peter is a very good dancer. Look at <u>him</u>.

Come and sit with <u>us</u>, Peter.

There's Alice. Go and talk with <u>her</u>.

OBJECT PRONOUNS	
Look at Peter.	Look at him.
Look at Maria.	Look at her.
Look at Barbara and Tino.	Look at them.
Look at Johnnie and me.	Look at us.
Look at the clock.	Look at it.

PRACTICE • *Make commands.*

Gladys is really strong.	That cat is incredible.
Look at her.	**Look at it.**

1. Tino is very happy.
2. Barbara is beautiful.
3. That dog is big.
4. Those girls are really tall.

5. Peter and I are good dancers.
6. Alice is a bad dancer.
7. Johnnie is sad.
8. Those flowers are very pretty.

WRITTEN EXERCISE • *Write sentences with object pronouns.*

Sit with Johnnie and me. *Sit with us*

1. Close the door. _____

2. Open the windows. _____

3. Talk with Alice. _____

4. Come with Barbara and me. _____

5. Dance with Peter. _____

6. Look at those girls. _____

7. Ask Maria. _____

8. Repeat the question. _____

Listen and repeat.

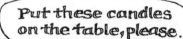

PRACTICE • *Give commands to other students in your class using these verbs:*

show	give	point (to)
put	bring	open
take	look at	close

Show me your watch.	**Give this pen to Nobu.**	**Point to the clock.**

PAIR WORK 1 • *Ask and answer questions.*

cards	pots
A: **Where are the cards?**	A: **Where are the pots?**
B: **They're on the floor.**	B: **They're on the wall.**

1. cups
2. pots
3. books
4. flowers
5. magazines
6. candles
7. glasses
8. oranges
9. dishes

PAIR WORK 2 • *Ask and answer questions.*

oranges/table?	dishes/table?
A: **Are the oranges on the table?**	A: **Are the dishes on the table?**
B: **Yes, they are.**	B: **No, they aren't. They're on the shelf.**

1. glasses/shelf?
2. candles/shelf?
3. magazines/chair?
4. books/chair?
5. dishes/shelf?
6. cups/table?
7. pots/floor?
8. cards/floor?

Listen and practice.

MR. BASCOMB: Good morning, Barbara.

BARBARA: Good morning, Mr. Bascomb. Here's a message from Mr. Grand.

MR. BASCOMB: Ah, yes. Please call him. Tell him the meeting is at ten o'clock.

BARBARA: Yes, sir. Is this an important meeting?

MR. BASCOMB: Very important. Mr. Grand is a big man in this city.

BARBARA: So are you, Mr. Bascomb.

MR. BASCOMB: Thanks, Barbara.

PAIR WORK • *Have conversations like the one on page 42.*

A: Good morning, _____.

B: Good morning, _____. Here's a message from _____.

A: Ah, yes. Please call _____. Tell _____ the meeting is at _____.

B: Yes, sir/ma'am.

1. Otis and Gloria
   them

2. Maria
   her

3. Johnnie
   him

4. Anne

5. Tino and
   Barbara

6. Nick

7. Fred and Barney

8. Mr. Moto

9. Mrs. Golo

Listen and repeat.

twenty-one

twenty-two

twenty-three

twenty-four

twenty-five

twenty-six

twenty-seven

twenty-eight

twenty-nine

thirty

forty

fifty

sixty

seventy

eighty

ninety

one hundred

two hundred ten

three hundred forty

four hundred sixty

🎧 *Listen and practice.*

MR. BASCOMB: That's a beautiful lamp.

SALESMAN: You're right.

MR. BASCOMB: How much is it?

SALESMAN: Seventy-eight dollars.

MR. BASCOMB: That's a good price. Here you are.

SALESMAN: Thank you. Have a nice day.

PAIR WORK • *Have similar conversations.*

A: That's a beautiful _____.

B: You're right.

A: How much is it?

B: _____ dollars.

A: That's a good price. Here you are.

B: Thank you. Have a nice day.

$78
1. lamp

$160
2. table

$45
3. chair

$300
4. desk

$225
5. easy chair

$480
6. sofa

$500
7. bed

$290
8. dresser

Listen and repeat.

1

It's six o'clock.

2

It's seven o'clock.

3

It's ten minutes past seven.
It's seven ten.

4

It's twenty minutes past seven.
It's seven twenty.

5

It's fifteen minutes past eight.
It's (a) quarter past eight.

6

It's thirty minutes past eight.
It's half past eight.

7

It's fifteen minutes to ten.
It's (a) quarter to ten.

8

It's five minutes to ten.

PAIR WORK • *Ask and answer questions.*

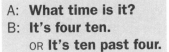

A: **What time is it?**
B: **It's four ten.**
 OR **It's ten past four.**

NEW VOCABULARY • TIMES OF DAY

 Listen and repeat.

It's noon.

It's midnight.

Morning is from
midnight to noon.

Afternoon is
from noon to six.

Evening is from
six to midnight.

Listen and practice.

STORY QUESTIONS

1. Why is Mrs. Golo worried?
2. What's her address?
3. Is her house far from the post office?
4. Is the post office on Lime Street?
5. Is it a big fire or a little one?
6. Is Mrs. Golo in the house now?
7. Is it dangerous?
8. What is the phone number for emergencies in the United States? in your country?

PRACTICE 1 • *Make commands.*

These glasses are dirty. (wash)	Maria isn't ready. (wait for)
Wash them.	**Wait for her.**

1. The door is open. (close)
2. There's Barbara. (talk to)
3. Tino is at home. (call)
4. I'm your friend. (listen to)
5. Here's Mrs. Golo. (ask)
6. Mr. and Mrs. Lee are in France. (write to)
7. Those are beautiful pictures. (look at)
8. Peter is a very good dancer. (dance with)

PRACTICE 2 • *Make commands. Use a verb with each of the words.*

book	**Open the book.** OR **Close the book.**
sentence	**Read the sentence.** OR **Repeat the sentence.**
Mrs. Golo	**Ask Mrs. Golo.** OR **Listen to Mrs. Golo.**

1. door
2. teacher
3. picture
4. Maria
5. magazine
6. window
7. letter
8. question
9. fire department

PAIR WORK • *Ask and answer questions about the picture on page 51. Use **between, next to,** and **across . . . from** in your answers.*

the State Bank/City Park	the Rex Theater/Mom's Cafe
A: **Excuse me, where's the State Bank?**	A: **Excuse me, where's the Rex Theater?**
B: **It's across the street from City Park.**	B: **It's next to Mom's Cafe.**
A: **Thank you.**	A: **Thank you.**

the barber shop/the flower shop and the supermarket
A: **Excuse me, where's the barber shop?**
B: **It's between the flower shop and the supermarket.**
A: **Thank you.**

1. the church/City Park
2. the parking lot/the supermarket and the Grand Hotel
3. the flower shop/the barber shop
4. the drug store/the church and the gas station
5. the Grand Hotel/Olson's Department Store
6. the gas station/the drug store
7. Mom's Cafe/the Rex Theater and the State Bank
8. the book store/the post office
9. the supermarket/the church

Give me your money!   Dance with me!   Take me to the airport!
Don't worry!   Don't sit down!   Don't leave me!
Eat your dinner!   Don't touch me!   Answer the phone!

Listen and practice.

PAIR WORK • *Have similar conversations.*

1. socks $6⁰⁰
2. dress   #98
3. shoes   #85
4. coat   #169
5. shirt   #45
6. pants   #80
7. sweater   #75
8. hat   #50

READING

Olson's Department Store is on Star Avenue. It's open every day from nine to five. It's a very good store. It's not expensive and the salespeople are very friendly.

FREE RESPONSE

1. What's the name of your favorite store?
2. Where is it?
3. What hours is the store open?
4. Is it expensive?
5. Are the salespeople friendly?

GRAMMAR SUMMARY

IMPERATIVE

Close the door!
Open the window!

Negative Imperative

| Don't | close the door! |
| | open the window! |

With Noun Objects

Look at	Peter.
	Maria.
	Barbara and Tino.
	Johnnie and me.
	the clock.

With Object Pronouns

Look at	him.
	her.
	them.
	us.
	it.

With Two Objects

Give	Jimmy	an apple.
	Linda	
	the children	
	Albert and me	
	the dog	

With Object Pronouns

Give	him	an apple.
	her	
	them	
	us	
	it	

TIME

What time is it?	It's	six	o'clock.
		seven	
		ten minutes	past seven.
		twenty minutes	
		(a) quarter	past eight.
		half	
		(a) quarter	to ten.
		five minutcs	

Question with HOW MUCH

| How much | is the watch? | It's twenty-five dollars. |
| | are the books? | They're ten dollars. |

Review Chapter

Listen and practice.

STORY QUESTIONS

1. Where is Mr. Wilson?
2. What time is it?
3. Who is Miss Tracy?
4. What is the dentist's name?
5. How are Mr. Wilson's teeth?
6. Where is the aspirin?
7. What is aspirin good for?
8. Where is the telephone?
9. Is the call for Miss Tracy?
10. Is Dr. Molar busy?
11. Is Mr. Wilson in good hands?
12. How much is Mr. Wilson's dental bill?
13. What is dental floss good for?
14. Is Miss Tracy a good nurse?

FREE RESPONSE

1. Is your dentist like Dr. Molar?
2. What is your dentist's name?
3. Where is your dentist's office?
4. Is your dentist cheap or expensive?
5. Are you afraid when you are at the dentist's?
6. Is sugar good or bad for your teeth?

WRITTEN EXERCISE • *Print your name, address, telephone number, and occupation.*

Please complete this form.

• PATIENT INFORMATION FORM •

name: Johnnie Wilson

address: 802 Oak Street
street

Wickam City
city

California 90720
state   zip

phone: 425-9063

occupation:
Businessman

• PATIENT INFORMATION FORM •

name: _____

address: _____
street

_____
city

_____
state   zip

phone: _____

occupation:

_____

A: Where are Joe and Eddie?
B: They're at the park.

A: Are they businessmen?
B: No, they aren't. (They're bums.)

A: Are they hot or cold?
B: They're cold.

A: Where's the cat?
B: It's in the tree.

A: Is it fat or thin?
B: It's fat.

A: Is it happy?
B: Yes, it is.

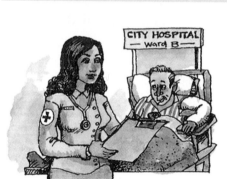

1. _____ Maria?

_____ a doctor or a teacher?

_____ ugly?

2. _____ Nick?

_____ a mechanic?

_____ old or young?

3. _____ Barbara and Anne?

_____ teachers or secretaries?

_____ busy?

4. _____ Tino?

_____ banker?

_____ tall or short?

5. _____ the clock?

_____ big or small?

_____ old?

6. _____ the apples?

_____ red or green?

_____ small?

7. _____ the woman?

_____ young or old?

_____ happy?

8. _____ the boys?

_____ friends?

_____ clean or dirty?

9. _____ Mr. and Mrs. Bascomb?

_____ rich or poor?

_____ afraid?

10. _____ the Mercedes?

_____ black or white?

_____ cheap?

 Listen and practice.

NANCY: Who's that?

GLORIA: His name's Tony Romero.

NANCY: He looks nice. Where's he from?

GLORIA: Spain.

NANCY: What's his occupation?

GLORIA: I'm not sure. I think he's a singer.

PAIR WORK • *Have similar conversations.*

A: Who's that?

B: _____.

A: He/she looks nice. Where's he/she from?

B: _____.

A: What's his/her occupation?

B: I'm not sure. I think he/she _____.

1. Laila Hassan/doctor

2. Nobu Moto/businessman

3. Fanta Mutombo/teacher

4. Diego Garcia/artist

5. Mary Wood/secretary

6. Ravi Patel/waiter

7. Natalya Romanov/dancer

8. Wong Wei/pilot

9. Antonia Morales/banker

PRACTICE • *Find the names on the menu.*

Number 1: **soda**

PAIR WORK 1 • *Ask about the prices.*

1: soda

A: **How much is a soda?**
B: **Seventy-five cents.**

Joe's Cafe

Hot Dog	$2.00
Hamburger	$3.50
Cheese Sandwich	$3.00
Soda	$.75
Orange Juice	$1.00
Coffee	$.60
Doughnut	$.75
Ice Cream	$1.50
Apple Pie	$2.00

CONVERSATION

Listen and practice.

Hello.

Hello. A cheese sandwich, please.

Anything else?

Yes, an orange juice.

PAIR WORK 2 • *Have similar conversations.*

A: Hello.

B: Hello. _____, please.

A: Anything else?

B: Yes, _____.
   OR No, that's all.

Listen and practice.

PAIR WORK • *Have similar conversations. Pay attention to street names.*

A: Take me to the Crest Theater.
B: On Rock Street?
A: No, it's on Dixon Avenue.
B: Here we are.
A: Thank you. How much is that?
B: Eleven dollars and forty-five cents.

1. Grand Hotel
   Baker Street?
   $9.25

2. State Bank
   Main Street?
   $8.30

3. post office
   Lime Street?
   $10.00

4. Rex Theater
   Sunset Avenue?
   $6.75

5. library
   Central Avenue?
   $7.90

6. hospital
   Dalton Avenue?
   $12.60

Listen and practice.

SANDY: One ticket to Los Angeles, please.

MR. LEE: One way or round trip?

SANDY: Round trip. How much?

MR. LEE: Seventy-five dollars and forty cents.

SANDY: When is the next bus?

MR. LEE: At seven-thirty.

PAIR WORK • *Have similar conversations.*

A: One ticket to _____, please.

B: One way or round trip?

A: _____. How much?

B: _____.

A: When is the next bus?

B: _____.

INFORMATION: DEPARTURES

Time • Destination
7:30 — Los Angeles
8:00 — San Francisco
8:25 — San Diego
9:10 — Portland
9:40 — Seattle
10:00 — Las Vegas
10:35 — Denver
11:10 — Chicago
11:45 — New York

1 Grayline Bus Company

from: Wickam City
to: Los Angeles

Ticket: Round Trip
Price: $75⁴⁰

2 Grayline Bus Company

from: Wickam City
to: San Francisco

Ticket: One Way
Price: $13⁰⁰

3 Grayline Bus Company

from: Wickam City
to: San Diego

Ticket: Round Trip
Price: $94²⁵

4 Grayline Bus Company

from: Wickam City
to: Portland

Ticket: One Way
Price: $51⁶⁵

5 Grayline Bus Company

from: Wickam City
to: Seattle

Ticket: Round Trip
Price: $188⁰⁰

6 Grayline Bus Company

from: Wickam City
to: Las Vegas

Ticket: One Way
Price: $32⁵⁰

7 Grayline Bus Company

from: Wickam City
to: Denver

Ticket: Round trip
Price: $209⁰⁰

8 Grayline Bus Company

from: Wickam City
to: Chicago

Ticket: One Way
Price: $176⁵⁰

9 Grayline Bus Company

from: Wickam City
to: New York

Ticket: Round trip
Price: $298⁰⁰

Come in!	Don't be afraid!	Sit down!
Don't talk!	Close the window!	Don't touch those cookies!
Hurry up!	Don't bring the cat!	Wait for me!

WRITTEN EXERCISE • *Complete the sentences using object pronouns: **her, him, it, them, me,** and **us.***

> Mr. Watkins is in his office. Take *him* this message.
>
> I'm your friend. Listen to *me* .

1. We're thirsty. Please bring _____ a bottle of soda.

2. That's a bad apple. Don't eat _____.

3. The dishes are dirty. Please wash _____.

4. Look! There's Mr. Bascomb. That's _____ over there.

5. His wife is in the hospital. Please take _____ these flowers.

6. Here's my phone number. Call _____ next week.

7. We aren't ready. Please wait for _____.

8. There's Peter and Maria. Let's talk with _____.

9. Maria is very pretty. Look at _____.

10. Peter is hungry. Bring _____ a sandwich.

11. Take the sandwich and put _____ on the table.

12. I'm very busy. Please help _____.

FREE RESPONSE

1. Are you hungry?
2. What is your favorite fruit?
3. Are oranges cheap or expensive?
4. Are apples good for you? soda?
5. How much is a bottle of soda?
6. How is your family?
7. Is your family at home now?
8. Where are your friends?
9. Where is your house/apartment?
10. What color is your room?
11. Is your street beautiful?
12. Where is the post office? library?
13. Is the post office open now? bank? library?
14. Are you busy in the morning?
15. What is your favorite animal?
16. Are you afraid of rats? spiders? snakes?

fruit

horse

lion

rat

spider

snake

1. _____ books are expensive.
   a. This   c. Those
   b. Them d. They

2. Where are the glasses?

   _____ on the shelf.
   a. They   c. There
   b. They're d. These

3. This is Miss Jones.

   _____ is a secretary.
   a. It   c. Her
   b. He   d. She

4. _____ is Nick? He's at the garage.
   a. Where c. Who
   b. What   d. How

5. _____ is that woman?

   She's Nancy Paine.
   a. Where c. What
   b. Who   d. How

6. What color is your car? It's _____.
   a. big   c. expensive
   b. new   d. red

7. Mr. Bascomb isn't poor.

   He's _____.
   a. happy c. rich
   b. tall   d. good

8. Those shoes aren't old.

   They're _____.
   a. new   c. big
   b. young d. cheap

9. Those are my post cards.

   Don't take _____.
   a. it   c. they
   b. that d. them

10. There's Maria. Let's talk with _____.
    a. him   c. her
    b. she   d. them

11. Call Mr. Poole. Give _____ the
    information.
    a. he   c. her
    b. him d. it

12. The tephone is _____ the living room.
    a. in   c. to
    b. on d. at

13. The girls are _____ the bus stop.
    a. in   c. to
    b. on d. at

14. Those men are tourists.

    They're _____ England.
    a. of   c. for
    b. from d. with

15. California is a beautiful _____.
    a. street c. state
    b. city   d. country

16. My _____ is 205 Oak Street.
    a. address   c. office
    b. telephone number d. business

17. How much are those magazines?
    a. They're on the table.
    b. There are five of them.
    c. They're two dollars each.
    d. They're three years old.

18. How old is that clock?
    a. It's twenty years old.
    b. It's two o'clock.
    c. It's two hundred dollars.
    d. It's expensive.

19. Aspirin is good for _____.
    a. work c. teeth
    b. pain d. dinner

20. New York is a _____ city.
    a. small   c. cheap
    b. English d. modern

(See page T-67 for answers.)

Chapter

5

TOPICS

Morning routines

Locations

Leisure activities

Colors

Clothes

GRAMMAR

Present continuous

Wh- questions

FUNCTIONS

Describing actions

Describing people's dress

Talking on the telephone

Listen and repeat.

It's Monday morning. Mr. and Mrs. Bascomb are getting up.

1. He's wearing pajamas.

2. She's wearing a nightgown.

3. He's brushing his teeth.

4. _____ her hair.

5. He's taking a shower.

6. _____ a bath.

7. He's making coffee.

8. _____ tea.

9. He's putting milk in his coffee.

10. _____ her tea.

11. He's reading a magazine.

12. _____ the newspaper.

13. He's eating an egg.

14. _____ an orange.

15. He's kissing his wife.

16. _____ her husband.

Listen and repeat.

1. Peter and Maria are sitting in a snack bar.

2. Barbara and Tino are sitting in a coffee shop.

3. They're watching a football game.

4. _____.

5. They're drinking soda.

6. _____.

7. They're talking to Otis.

8. _____.

9. They're playing darts.

10. _____.

11. They're looking at the clock.

12. _____.

13. They're paying the cashier.

14. _____.

15. They're saying "good-bye" to Otis.

16. _____.

1. A: Where's Mr. Bascomb?
   B: He's in the bathroom.
   A: What's he doing?
   B: He's taking a shower.

2. A: Where are Barbara and Tino?
   B: They're at Mom's Cafe.
   A: What are they doing?
   B: They're drinking coffee.

3. _____ Anne?

   _____ doing?

4. _____ Fred and Barney?

   _____ doing?

5. _____ Jimmy and Linda?

   _____ doing?

6. _____ Mrs. Bascomb?

   _____ doing?

7. _____ Nick?

   _____ doing?

8. _____ Otis and Gloria?

   _____ doing?

1

2

1. *Talk about the pictures.*
2. *Listen to the stories.*
3. *Answer the story questions.*

READING

1 It's Saturday night at the Student Club. Jimmy and Linda are dancing and Tony's watching them. Albert's standing by the table. He's eating a sandwich. Bill and Jane are talking to each other and Karen's walking to the door. It's eleven o'clock and she's going home.

1. What night is it?
2. What are Jimmy and Linda doing? (b)
3. What's Tony doing? (a)
4. Where's Albert standing? (c)
5. What's he eating?
6. What are Bill and Jane doing? (d)
7. What's Karen doing? (e)
8. Where's she going?

2 Sam and Mabel Brown are in a small restaurant. They're sitting at a table in the corner. Sam's calling the waiter and Mabel's looking at the menu. The waiter's standing at the counter. He's reading a newspaper.

1. Where are Sam and Mabel?
2. Are they standing or sitting?
3. Who's Sam calling?
4. What's Mabel looking at?
5. Where's the waiter?
6. What's he doing?

PRESENT CONTINUOUS Affirmative	
Karen's walking to the door.	We're reading the newspaper.
She's _____ .	They're _____ .
John's _____ .	You're _____ .
He's _____ .	I'm _____ .

PAIR WORK • *Ask and answer questions about the stories.*

A: Is Albert eating an apple? (a sandwich)
B: **No, he's eating a sandwich.**

1
1. Is Linda dancing with Albert? (with Jimmy)
2. Is Tony watching Karen? (Jimmy and Linda)
3. Is Karen walking to the table? (to the door)
4. Is she going to a movie? (home)
5. Is she wearing a long dress? (a short dress)

2
1. Are Sam and Mabel sitting in a coffee shop? (in a restaurant)
2. Is Mabel looking at Sam? (at the menu)
3. Is Sam calling the cashier? (the waiter)
4. Is the waiter standing by the table? (by the counter)
5. Is he reading a magazine? (a newspaper)

Listen and practice.

ALBERT: Hi, Jimmy. Where's your sister?

JIMMY: At home. She's helping my mother.

ALBERT: Is she washing the dishes?

JIMMY: No, she isn't.

ALBERT: What's she doing?

JIMMY: She's cleaning the windows.

ALBERT: Is your father home?

JIMMY: Yes. He's cutting the grass.

ALBERT: Why aren't you working, too?

JIMMY: It's Sunday. I'm resting today.

1. **Linda is cleaning the windows.
   She isn't cleaning the floor.**

2. **Jimmy and Albert are talking about Linda.
   They aren't talking about Karen.**

3. Otis is reading a newspaper.
   _____ a magazine.

4. Mr. and Mrs. Bascomb are having breakfast.
   _____ dinner.

5. Barbara and Tino are drinking lemonade.
   _____ orange juice.

6. Jenny is wearing jeans.
   _____ a dress.

7. Peter is dancing with Maria.
   _____ with Nancy.

8. The women are playing baseball.
   _____ basketball.

It's a beautiful Sunday. The sun is shining and the birds are singing. The Brown family is in the park. Sam and Mabel are preparing lunch. Sam is cooking hot dogs. Mabel is making sandwiches and lemonade. Linda is sitting by a tree drawing pictures. Jimmy is playing football. An old man is sitting on the hill watching the game. He's smiling and thinking about the past.

STORY QUESTIONS

1. Where is the Brown family?
2. Are Sam and Mabel preparing lunch?
3. Is Sam cooking hamburgers?
4. What is Mabel making?

5. Where is Linda?
6. What's she doing?
7. Is Jimmy playing basketball?
8. What is the old man doing?

PAIR WORK • *Ask and answer questions using these verbs:* **buy, eat, drink, make, play, read, watch,** *and* **wear.**

1. Mabel/sandwiches?
A: **Is Mabel making sandwiches?**
B: **Yes, she is.**

2. the boys/basketball?
A: **Are the boys playing basketball?**
B: **No, they aren't. They're playing football.**

3. Linda/a pear?

4. Otis and Gloria/TV?

5. Maria/a green dress?

6. Fred and Barney/lemonade?

7. Mr. Moto/a newspaper?

8. Mr. and Mrs. Golo/a clock?

9. Anne/a piano?

red   orange   yellow   green   blue   brown   beige   gray   white

PAIR WORK 1 • *Ask and answer questions about the people in the picture.*

1. Jenny
A: **What is Jenny wearing?**
B: **She's wearing a yellow blouse and a red skirt.**

2. Marty
A: **What is Marty wearing?**
B: **He's wearing a white shirt and blue pants.**

PAIR WORK 2 • *Ask and answer the same question about the other students in your class.*

WRITTEN EXERCISE • *Listen to the story about the picture. Listen again and write the story.*

PAIR WORK 3 • *Ask and answer questions about the picture.*

A: **What are Jenny and Marty doing?**
B: **They're waving to Barbara and Tino.**

Listen and practice.

JACK: Hi, Sam. What are you doing?

SAM: I'm working. What are you doing?

JACK: Nothing . . . just relaxing.

SAM: Oh, what a sweet life!

PAIR WORK • *Have similar conversations.*

A: Hi, _____. What are you doing?

B: _____. What are you doing?

A: Nothing . . . just relaxing.

B: Oh, what a sweet life!

PRESENT CONTINUOUS Affirmative

He She It	's (is)	
I	'm (am)	watching television.
You We They	're (are)	

Negative

He She It	isn't (is not) 's not	
I	'm not (am not)	watching television.
You We They	aren't (are not) 're not	

Interrogative

Is	he she it	
Am	I	watching television?
Are	you we they	

Short Answers

Yes,	he she it	is.	No,	he she it	isn't.
	I	am.		I	'm not.
	you we they	are.		you we they	aren't.

Questions with WHAT, WHO, WHERE

What	's (is) Albert eating?	A sandwich.
Who	's (is) Linda dancing with?	Jimmy.
Where	's (is) Sam going?	To the garage.

Chapter

TOPICS
Physical characteristics
Small talk

GRAMMAR
"To have"
Possessive adjectives
Possessive of nouns
"Whose . . . ?"

FUNCTIONS
Identifying possessions
Describing people
Getting and giving personal information

CARTOON STORY

TO HAVE Affirmative

Louie has a great car.	You have good friends.
He _____.	They _____.
Nancy _____.	We _____.
She _____.	I _____.

WRITTEN EXERCISE • *Complete the sentences with* **have** *or* **has.**

Barney *has* a red taxi.

Mr. and Mrs. Brown *have* a large refrigerator.

1. They _____ a friend named Jack.

2. He _____ two brothers.

3. You _____ a nice family.

4. Tino _____ a girlfriend named Barbara.

5. She _____ a beautiful smile.

6. I _____ a new radio.

7. We _____ a good library.

8. Mrs. Bascomb _____ a rich husband.

9. He _____ an important job.

10. They _____ an expensive car.

a refrigerator

a radio

PAIR WORK • *Ask and answer questions.*

> a brother
> A: **Do you have a brother?**
> B: **Yes, I do.** OR **No, I don't.**

1. a sister
2. a clock
3. a watch
4. a cat
5. a dog
6. a guitar
7. a computer
8. a camera
9. a football
10. a bicycle

a computer

a camera

Listen and practice.

ANNE: Barbara, give me your pen, please.

BARBARA: I don't have a pen. Here's a pencil.

ANNE: Thank you. Do you have a piece of paper?

BARBARA: Here you are. Is it for a letter?

ANNE: That's right. Do you have an envelope?

BARBARA: Yes. But I don't have stamps.

ANNE: That's OK, I have stamps.

BARBARA: Oh, really? That's good.

TO HAVE Interrogative	
Do you have an envelope?	Does Anne have a pen?
_____ they _____?	_____ she _____?
_____ we _____?	_____ John _____?
_____ the girls _____?	_____ he _____?

WRITTEN EXERCISE 1 • *Complete the questions with **do** or **does**.*

Do they have a computer?
Does Albert have a telephone?

a telephone   a computer

1. _____ we have a dictionary?

2. _____ she have a bicycle?

3. _____ you have a sister?

4. _____ I have your address?

5. _____ Nick have a garage?

6. _____ you have a guitar?

7. _____ Maria have a brown hat?

8. _____ they have an apartment?

9. _____ he have a lamp?

10. _____ we have stamps?

TO HAVE Negative	
We don't have a clock.	Linda doesn't have a car.
They _____.	She _____.
You _____.	Jimmy _____.
I _____.	He _____.

WRITTEN EXERCISE 2 • *Complete the sentences with **don't** or **doesn't**.*

They *don't* have a piano.
Joe *doesn't* have a television.

a piano   a television (TV)

1. We _____ have a computer.

2. Barbara _____ have a pen.

3. I _____ have a dictionary.

4. They _____ have a telephone.

5. He _____ have a camera.

6. You _____ have an umbrella.

7. I _____ have a bicycle.

8. She _____ have a car.

9. Louie _____ have a girlfriend.

10. We _____ have your phone number.

PAIR WORK 1 • *Ask and answer questions.*

1. A: **Does Tino have a wallet?**
   B: **Yes, he does.**

2. A: **Does Mrs. Bascomb have a wallet?**
   B: **No, she doesn't. She has a handbag.**

3. Does Maria have a bottle?

4. Does Barbara have a computer?

5. Does Albert have an apple?

6. Does Simon have a rabbit?

7. Does Mrs. Golo have an umbrella?

8. Does Barney have a truck?

9. Does Anne have a guitar?

PAIR WORK 2 • *Ask your partner if the other students have these things:*
pen, pencil, dictionary, watch, handbag, umbrella, hat.

A: **Does Pedro have a dictionary?**
B: **Yes, he does.** OR **No, he doesn't.***

*If you aren't sure, ask him if he has a dictionary.

PAIR WORK • *Ask and answer questions.*

A: Do Mr. and Mrs. Wankie have a house?
B: **No, they don't. (They have an apartment.)**

A: Do they have a telephone?
B: **Yes, they do.**

1. Do they have a radio?
2. Do they have a piano?
3. Do they have a clock?
4. Do they have a bookcase?
5. Do they have a computer?
6. Do they have a camera?
7. Do they have a television?
8. Do they have a dog?
9. Do they have a cat?

Listen and repeat.

POSSESSIVE ADJECTIVES	
I have a book.	It's **my** book.
You have a book.	It's **your** book.
He has a book.	It's **his** book.
She has a book.	It's **her** book.
We have a book.	It's **our** book.
They have a book.	It's **their** book.

WRITTEN EXERCISE 1 • *Complete the sentences with* **my, your, his, her, our,** *or* **their.**

Peter has a clock in ____*his*____ apartment.

1. Maria has a piano in _____ apartment.

2. Mr. and Mrs. Brown have a television in _____ living room.

3. I have an umbrella in _____ car.

4. We have a good library in _____ city.

5. She has a radio in _____ room.

6. You have a beautiful vase in _____ kitchen.

7. I have a pen in _____ pocket.

8. He has a newspaper in _____ desk.

WRITTEN EXERCISE 2 • *Complete the sentences.*

They're painting ____*their*____ house.

1. I'm waiting for _____ sister.

2. She's talking with _____ friends.

3. They're doing _____ homework.

4. Is Jimmy helping _____ mother?

5. Linda is talking with _____ father.

6. He's cleaning _____ shoes.

7. Are you thinking about _____ family?

8. We're thinking about _____ friends.

CONVERSATION

 Listen and practice.

JIMMY: Whose car is that?

ALBERT: It's Mr. Smith's car.

PAIR WORK • *Ask and answer questions.*

1. A: **Whose house is that?**
   B: **It's the Golos' house.**

2. A: **Whose glasses are these?**
   B: **They're Anne's glasses.**

3. Whose _____ is this?
   _____ Barney's _____.

4. Whose _____ are those?
   _____ the boys' _____.

5. Whose _____ is this?
   _____ Maria's _____.

6. Whose _____ is that?
   _____ the Brown's _____.

7. Whose _____ are these?
   _____ Jimmy's _____.

8. Whose _____ is this?
   _____ Sam's _____.

9. Whose _____ are those?
   _____ the girls' _____.

Mr. Brown is a family man. He has a wife, Mabel, and two children. Their names are Jimmy and Linda. The Browns have a small house with a red roof. Their house is near the library. Mr. Brown has a car and his wife also has a car. His car is orange and her car is blue. Right now, Mr. Brown is washing his car. His dog, Fenwick, is at his side. Mrs. Brown is working in the garden. She's planting vegetables. Linda is helping her mother in the garden. Jimmy isn't home. He's playing football with his friends.

STORY QUESTIONS

1. Does Mr. Brown have children?
2. What are their names?
3. Do the Browns have a big house with a white roof?
4. Where is their house?
5. Do Mr. and Mrs. Brown have small cars?
6. What color is his car?
7. What color is her car?
8. Do the Browns have a dog or a cat?
9. What's the dog's name?
10. What's Mr. Brown doing now?
11. What's Mrs. Brown doing?
12. What's Linda doing?
13. Is Jimmy helping, too?

PAIR WORK • *Ask and answer questions.*

1. Barbara/hand

A: **What does Barbara have in her hand?**
B: **She has a mirror.**

2. cat/mouth

A: **What does the cat have in its mouth?**
B: **It has a fish.**

3. Golos/garage

A: **What do the Golos have in their garage?**
B: **They have a sailboat.**

4. Johnny/pocket

5. dog/mouth

6. Anne/handbag

7. Bascombs/living room

8. Simon/hat

9. Jenny/hand

DESCRIBING PEOPLE

Listen and repeat.

Barbara has
blond hair.

Nancy has
brown hair.

Suzi has
black hair.

Barney is
short.

Otis is
average
height.

Mr. Poole
is tall.

Linda is
about twenty.

Sam is in
his forties.

Mrs. Morley is
in her seventies.

PRACTICE • *Describe these people.*

Number 1: Barbara **She's *short*, she has *blond hair*, and she's *about twenty-five*.**

1. Barbara   2. Mr. Poole   3. Sam   4. Barney   5. Miss Hackey   6. Suzi   7. Mrs. Morley

FREE RESPONSE

1. Describe someone in your family.
2. Describe your best friend.
3. Describe a famous person.
4. Describe your favorite movie star.
5. Describe the president of the United States.

SMALL TALK

WRITTEN EXERCISE • *Write a question for each answer.*

1. What's your name? — My name is Nobu.

2. [   ] — I'm from Tokyo.

3. [   ] — My favorite singer is Michael Jackson.

4. [   ] — It's nine o'clock.

5. [   ] — I'm going home.

6. [   ] — My phone number is 260-5347.

7. [   ] — That woman is Maria Miranda.

8. [   ] — She's a doctor.

9. [   ] — She's twenty-seven.

FREE RESPONSE

1. What nationality are you?
2. What city are you from?
3. What's it like?
4. How is your family?
5. Do you have any brothers or sisters?
6. Where are they?
7. What are they doing now?
8. Are you having a good time?
9. Are you thirsty?
10. What is your favorite drink?

ROLE PLAY • *You're at a party. Introduce yourself to four people. Ask them some of the questions above and ask some original questions.*

TO HAVE Affirmative

He She	has	
I You We They	have	a car.

Negative

He She	doesn't (does not)	
I You We They	don't (do not)	have a car.

Interrogative

Does	he she	
Do	I you we they	have a car?

Short Answers

Yes,	he she	does.	No,	he she	doesn't.
	I you we they	do.		I you we they	don't.

POSSESSIVE ADJECTIVES

It's	my your our their his her	house.

Questions with WHOSE

Whose	radio is this? pens are these?
Whose	house is that? bicycles are those?

POSSESSIVE OF NOUNS

It's Mrs. Golo's radio.
They're Linda's pens.

It's the Browns' house.
They're the girls' bicycles.

Chapter 7

TOPICS
Food and drinks
The home and furniture

GRAMMAR
There is/there are
Some/any
Countables and uncountables
"To like," "to want," "to need"

FUNCTIONS
Asking about quantity
Expressing preferences in food
Expressing satisfaction/dissatisfaction
Expressing likes/dislikes
Expressing want-desire
Expressing need

 *Listen and repeat.*

There's a dog under the table.

_____ chair by the table.

_____ typewriter on the table.

_____ lamp behind the typewriter.

_____ vase next to the typewriter.

_____ rose in the vase.

_____ cup in the front of the vase.

PRACTICE • *Answer the questions about the picture.*

Is there a typewriter on the table?	Is there a book on the table?
Yes, there is.	**No, there isn't.**

1. Is there a cup on the table?
2. Is there a glass on the table?
3. Is there a bottle on the table?
4. Is there a vase on the table?
5. Is there a rose in the vase?

6. Is there a chair by the table?
7. Is there a magazine on the chair?
8. Is there a dog under the table?
9. Is there a cat under the table?

PAIR WORK • *Ask and answer questions about your classroom.*

flag
A: **Is there a flag in the room?**
B: **Yes, there is.**
OR **No, there isn't.**

flag   map

1. clock
2. television
3. computer
4. wastebasket
5. radio
6. map
7. flag
8. calendar
9. newspaper
10. table

·JANUARY·

Sunday	Monday	Tuesday	Wednesday	Thursday	Friday	Saturday
		1	2	3	4	5
6	7	8	9	10	11	12

calendar

Listen and repeat.

There are some cars in the street.

_____ people at the bus stop.

_____ birds on the sidewalk.

_____ bicycles under the tree.

_____ children in front of the theater.

_____ tables and chairs on the sidewalk.

PRACTICE • *Answer the questions about the picture.*

> Are there any cars in the street?
> **Yes, there are.**
>
> Are there any buses in the street?
> **No, there aren't.**

1. Are there any trucks in the street?
2. Are there any people at the bus stop?
3. Are there any people at Joe's Cafe?
4. Are there any birds on the sidewalk?
5. Are there any birds in the tree?
6. Are there any bicycles under the tree?
7. Are there any tables and chairs on the sidewalk?
8. Are there any glasses on the tables?
9. Are there any children in front of the theater?

PAIR WORK • *Ask and answer questions.*

> A: How many days are there in a week?
> B: **There are seven days in a week.**

1. How many months are there in a year?
2. How many hours are there in a day?
3. How many minutes are there in an hour?
4. How many people are there in your family?
5. How many chapters are there in this book?
6. How many pages are there in this book?

PRACTICE 1 • Complete the sentences.

There's a bus in the street. **It's a** school bus.

1. _____ garden in the front yard. _____ vegetable garden.
2. _____ fence around the garden. _____ wire fence.
3. _____ table near the garden. _____ picnic table.

There are some cans on the sidewalk. **They're** trash cans.

1. _____ trees next to the house. _____ peach trees.
2. _____ cartons on the table. _____ milk cartons.
3. _____ boots on the steps. _____ cowboy boots.

PRACTICE 2 • Answer the questions about the picture.

What's in the street?
There's a bus in the street.

What's on the sidewalk?
There are some cans on the sidewalk.

What kind of bus is it?
It's a school bus.

What kind of cans are they?
They're trash cans.

1. What's next to the house?
   What kind of trees are they?

2. What's in the front yard?
   What kind of garden is it?

3. What's around the garden?
   What kind of fence is it?

4. What's near the garden?
   What kind of table is it?

5. What's on the table?
   What kind of cartons are they?

6. What's on the steps?
   What kind of boots are they?

UNCOUNTABLES

There's some bread on the table.
_____ cheese _____ .
_____ butter _____ .
_____ milk _____ .

PAIR WORK • _Ask and answer questions._

1. a carton of milk

2. a box of cereal

3. a pitcher of lemonade

A: **What's in the carton?**
B: **There's some milk in the carton.**

4. a bowl of soup

5. a cup of coffee

6. a dish of ice cream

7. a jar of mustard

8. a bag of rice

9. a can of tomato juice

GROUP WORK • _Think of five uncountable food items that aren't on this page and make a list. Make another list of five countable food items. They can be items in your kitchen or in the market._

Uncountable food item: **sugar**   Countable food item: **apple**

WRITTEN EXERCISE • *Complete the sentences using **there's a**, **there's some**, or **there are some**.*

There's a _____ plate on the table.
There are some _____ cookies on the plate.

1. _____ coffeepot on the table.

   _____ coffee in the coffeepot.

2. _____ bread on the table.

   _____ knives next to the bread.

3. _____ bottle on the table.

   _____ orange juice in the bottle.

4. _____ sandwiches on the table.

   _____ cheese next to the sandwiches.

5. _____ dish on the table.

   _____ cherries in the dish.

Note: knife ⟶ knives   wife ⟶ wives   life ⟶ lives

WRITTEN EXERCISE • *Fill in the blanks with **bag, bottle, box, bunch, can,** or **jar**.*

1.

a _bunch_ of bananas

2.

a _jar_ of olives

3.

a _bag_ of potatoes

4.

a _____ of orange juice

5.

a _____ of corn flakes

6.

a _____ of cherry soda

7.

a _____ of apples

8.

a _____ of carrots

9.

a _____ of cookies

10.

a _____ of onion soup

11.

a _____ of ketchup

12.

a _____ of mayonnaise

Listen and repeat.

PAIR WORK I • *Talk about food.*

ham	hot dogs
fish	hamburgers
chicken	spaghetti
roast beef	pizza

A: What do you like?

B: I like _____. What

about you?

A: I like _____.

PAIR WORK 2 • *Talk about drinks.*

coffee	orange juice
tea	lemonade
milk	cherry soda

A: Do you like _____?

B: Yes, I do.

OR No, I don't. I prefer _____.

GROUP WORK • *Work in groups of four or five. One student asks the other students to name their favorite food and drink. What is the most popular food and drink in your group? Tell the class.*

Listen and repeat.

PAIR WORK • *Ask and answer questions about the customers in Mom's Cafe. Use the verb to like.*

1. Suzi
A: **What does Suzi like?**
B: **She likes apple pie.**

2. Otis and Gloria
A: **What do Otis and Gloria like?**
B: **They like lemonade.**

3. Johnnie
4. Barney and Fred
5. Anne
6. Mr. and Mrs. Farley
7. Jenny and Marty
8. Mr. Bascomb
9. Maria

Listen and practice.

ROLE PLAY • *You are in a restaurant. Student A (waiter or waitress) asks Student B (customer) what he or she wants for lunch. The customer chooses from the following:*

coffee	ham sandwich	mayonnaise
milk	cheese sandwich	mustard
orange juice	roast beef sandwich	ketchup
lemonade	hot dog	
cherry soda	hamburger	

A: What do you want for lunch, _____?

B: I want some _____ and a _____.

A: Do you want _____ on your _____?

B: Yes, please. OR No, thanks. I don't like _____.

Listen and repeat.

CONVERSATION

 Listen and practice.

PAIR WORK • *Have similar conversations. Choose any vegetables.*

A: What do you need today, _____?

B: I need some _____ and _____.

A: Do you need any _____?

B: No, I already have some, thank you.

FREE RESPONSE

1. Which market do you go to?

2. What kind of food do you buy?

PAIR WORK 1 • *The people in the pictures are making salads. Ask and answer questions about them.*

1. Tino
A: **What vegetables is Tino using for his salad?**
B: **He's using cucumbers, mushrooms, peppers, and radishes.**

Vegetables	
carrots	onions
cucumbers	peppers
lettuce	radishes
mushrooms	tomatoes

1. Tino

2. Suzi

3. Otis

4. Maria

PAIR WORK 2 • *Ask and answer questions.*

A: **Whose salad do you like best?**
B: **Maria's salad.***
A: **Why?**
B: **Because it has carrots and radishes, and I love carrots and radishes.**

*If you don't like salad, say "I don't like any of them."

GROUP WORK • *Talk about vegetables.*

1. Do you like vegetables?
2. What's your favorite vegetable?
3. Are there any vegetables you don't like?
4. Which vegetables do you use for salad?
5. Where do you buy vegetables?
6. Do you have a vegetable garden?

There's an old white house on Bunker Hill. It's a traditional American house. It has large windows and a wide green door. There's a statue of a woman in front of the house. And there are red roses in the garden. The trees behind the house are tall and very beautiful. The house belongs to an old professor. He's a butterfly expert. His name is Dr. Pasto. The people of Bunker Hill like him because he's very friendly. He has visitors every day. At the moment, Dr. Pasto is chasing butterflies. He wants them for his collection.

STORY QUESTIONS

1. Describe Dr. Pasto's house. Is it old or new? What color is it?
2. Is there a statue of a man in front of the house?
3. What kind of flowers are in the garden?
4. Where are the trees? What are they like?
5. What is Dr. Pasto doing now?
6. Why do people like Dr. Pasto?
7. How old do you think he is?
8. Do you like Dr. Pasto's house? Why?

PRACTICE • *Answer the questions about the picture.*

What's in the bathroom? (a mirror)
There's a mirror in the bathroom.
What's in the bedroom? (some flowers)
There are some flowers in the bedroom.

1. What's in the kitchen? (a stove)
   (some pots)
   (a sink)

2. What's in the living room? (some chairs)
   (a table)
   (a television)

3. What's in the bathroom? (a bathtub)
   (a toilet)
   (a wash basin)

4. What's in the bedroom? (a bed)
   (some flowers)
   (a picture)

PAIR WORK 1 • *Ask and answer questions about the picture on page 114.*

pots/kitchen	television/bedroom
A: **Are there any pots in the kitchen?**	A: **Is there a television in the bedroom?**
B: **Yes, there are.**	B: **No, there isn't.**

1. window/bedroom
2. window/bathroom
3. mirror/bathroom
4. chairs/living room
5. chairs/bedroom
6. table/bedroom
7. flowers/bedroom
8. flowers/living room
9. sofa/living room

PAIR WORK 2 • *Ask and answer questions about the contents of the refrigerator.*

milk

A: **Is there any milk in the refrigerator?**
B: **Yes, there is.**

bananas

A: **Are there any bananas in the refrigerator?**
B: **No, there aren't.**

1. cheese
2. butter
3. eggs
4. bread
5. cake
6. cookies
7. ice cream
8. apples
9. cherries
10. pears
11. lemonade
12. orange juice

PRACTICE 1 • *Make affirmative sentences with* **to want.**

Anne likes cake. (a piece)	We like lemonade. (a glass)
She wants a piece of cake.	**We want a glass of lemonade.**

1. Johnnie likes French fries. (a plate)
2. Fred and Barney like coffee. (a cup)
3. Maria likes cheese. (a piece)
4. I like tomato soup. (a bowl)
5. Peter likes spaghetti. (a plate)
6. We like ice cream. (a dish)
7. They like orange juice. (a glass)
8. Barbara likes tea. (a cup)

PRACTICE 2 • *Make negative sentences with* **to like** *and* **to want.**

I/coffee
I don't like coffee. I don't want any (coffee).

Otis/ham
Otis doesn't like ham. He doesn't want any (ham).

1. Gloria/tomato soup
2. We/French fries
3. They/onions
4. Johnnie/olives
5. I/cheese
6. My friends/pizza
7. Mr. Farley/chicken
8. We/string beans

PAIR WORK • *Ask and answer questions using **have**, **like**, and **want**.*

1. Mr. Bascomb/a secretary?

A: **Does Mr. Bascomb have a secretary?**
B: **Yes, he does.**

2. Anne/her job?

A: **Does Anne like her job?**
B: **No, she doesn't.**

3. Anne/a raise?

A: **Does Anne want a raise?**
B: **Yes, she does.**

have   4. Peter/a car?   5. Joe and Eddie/a car?   6. Joe and Eddie/money?

like 7. Barbara and Tino/rock music? 8. Mr. Bascomb/rock music? 9. Mrs. Bascomb/ice cream?

want   10. Jenny/ice cream?   11. Barbara and Tino/ice cream?   12. Barbara and Tino/soda?

FREE RESPONSE 1

1. Are you thirsty? Do you want a glass of water?
2. Are you hungry? Do you want a sandwich?
3. Do you like ice cream? cake?
4. Do you like lemonade? coffee?
5. What's your favorite food? drink?
6. What's your favorite sport?
7. Do you like football? basketball? baseball?
8. Is baseball popular in your country?
9. Who is your favorite athlete?
10. What's your favorite team?

a baseball game

WRITTEN EXERCISE • *Complete the sentences using suitable prepositions.*

Barbara is sitting _with_ Tino _in_ his car.

1. She's talking _____ her job _____ the bank.

2. Albert and Linda are sitting _____ a coffee shop.

3. She wants a bowl _____ soup _____ lunch.

4. Jimmy is buying some stamps _____ the post office _____ Maple Street.

5. He's writing a letter _____ a friend _____ Florida.

6. The post office is open _____ nine _____ five.

7. That old house belongs _____ Dr. Pasto.

8. He's working _____ the garden.

9. I'm giving this butterfly _____ Dr. Pasto _____ his collection.

FREE RESPONSE 2

1. How old is your house or apartment?
2. How many rooms are there? Are they large or small?
3. What is your living room like? How many windows are there?
4. What color are the walls? Are there any pictures on the walls?
5. Are there any plants or flowers in your home?
6. What is the kitchen like? Is it large or small?
   Is it next to the living room?
7. What is the furniture like? Is it comfortable?
8. Do you have a balcony? a fireplace?
9. What do you need for your house or apartment?
10. What's the best thing about your home?

a balcony

a fireplace

THERE IS/THERE ARE Affirmative

There's (There is)	a bottle	
There are	some glasses	on the table.
There's (There is)	some cake	

Negative

There isn't (There is not)	a bottle	
There aren't (There are not)	any glasses	on the table.
There's isn't (There is not)	any cake	

Interrogative

Is there	a bottle	
Are there	any glasses	on the table?
Is there	any cake	

Short Answers

	there is.			there isn't.
Yes,	there are.	No,		there aren't.
	there is.			there isn't.

NOUNS AS MODIFIERS

It's a	school bus. business letter.
They're	apple trees. office buildings.

TO WANT Affirmative

He She	wants	
I You We They	want	a glass of water.

Negative

He She	doesn't (does not)	
I You We They	don't (do not)	want a glass of water.

Interrogative

Does	he she	
Do	I you we they	want a glass of water?

Short Answers

	he she	does.		he she	doesn't.
Yes,	I you we they	do.	No,	I you we they	don't.

Review Chapter

TOPICS
Art exhibition
Popular entertainment
A trip to Paris
Leisure activities

GRAMMAR
Review

FUNCTIONS

Expressing preferences in entertainment
Indicating location
Describing actions
Making suggestions
Offering to help
Expressing need
Apologizing
Expressing disappointment
Expressing gratitude

Today there's an art exhibition in City Park. Otis Jackson has some of his new paintings in the exhibition. He's showing them to the public for the first time. Otis is a very good artist. His paintings are an expression of his strong personality. He's a vegetarian; that's why Otis likes to paint fruit and vegetables. The fruit and vegetables in Otis's paintings are different from ordinary fruit and vegetables. They're very large and have strange shapes and colors.

At the moment Otis is talking to some art lovers, including Dr. Pasto. They're standing around some of his paintings of fruit. Otis is a good talker, and he has some interesting ideas on art.

"Art is life," says Otis. "My paintings are me."

"That's certainly true," says Dr. Pasto. "You and your paintings are very original."

"Thank you, Dr. Pasto."

"This is a fine painting here, Otis. The colors are beautiful."

"You're looking at one of my favorite compositions. It's called 'The Happy Butterfly.'"

"Is it for sale, Otis?"

"Yes, sir."

"How much do you want for it?"

"I'm asking eighty dollars."

"Let's see. I think I have eighty dollars in my wallet. Yes. Here you are, Otis."

"Thank you, Dr. Pasto. You have a good painting there. Enjoy it."

STORY QUESTIONS

1. Where is the art exhibition?
2. Is Otis showing his new paintings today?
3. Why does Otis like to paint fruit and vegetables?
4. Who is Otis talking to?
5. What does Otis say about art?
6. What is Dr. Pasto looking at?
7. What is the painting called?
8. Why does Dr. Pasto like the painting?
9. How much does Otis want for it? Is that a good price?
10. Do you think Otis is a good artist?
11. Do you like to paint? Are you a good artist?

Listen and repeat.

MOVIES: musicals, comedies, westerns, science fiction, dramas.

TV PROGRAMS: dramas, news, sports, cartoons, comedies.

MUSIC: rock, jazz, country western, classical, popular.

BOOKS: mysteries, love stories, biographies, historical books.

PAIR WORK 1 • *Look at page 122. Ask and answer questions about movies, TV programs, music, and books.*

A: **What kind of movies do you like?**
B: **I like comedies and dramas.**

A: **What's your favorite movie?**
B: **Star Wars.**

PAIR WORK 2 • *Ask and answer questions.*

A: **Is Peter married?**
B: **No, he isn't. He's single.**

A: **Are Barbara and Tino nice people?**
B: **Yes, they are.**

1. Is Mr. Bascomb a banker?
2. Is he poor?
3. Are Jimmy and Linda old?
4. Are they students?
5. Are you a tourist?
6. Are you very busy today?
7. Is the post office open now?
8. Are London and Tokyo small cities?
9. Is the United States a big country?
10. Is it hot in Iceland?

WRITTEN EXERCISE • *Complete the sentences using object pronouns.*

There's Maria. Let's talk with *her*.
I'm coming. Wait for *me*.

1. Call the waiter. Ask _____ for the menu.

2. We're thirsty. Please bring _____ some water.

3. That apple is no good. Don't eat _____.

4. Those aren't your magazines. Don't take _____.

5. Here's my telephone number. Call _____ tonight.

6. We don't have the school's address. Please give _____ to _____.

7. The students are in the classroom. Mrs. Golo is with _____.

8. Mrs. Golo is a good teacher. The students like _____.

9. Where's my dictionary? Do you have _____?

10. Marty has chocolate on his face. Look at _____.

PRACTICE • *Answer the questions about the picture.*

1. How many dogs are there in the street?
2. How many firefighters are there on the fire truck?
3. How many children are there in front of the snack bar?
4. How many police officers are there in the street?
5. How many passengers are there in Barney's taxi?
6. How many bicycles are there in front of the movie theater?
7. How many cats are there on the roof?
8. How many birds are there in the picture?
9. How many trees are there in the picture?

WRITTEN EXERCISE • *Answer the questions about the picture.*

Where are the dogs? _*They're in*_ the street.

Where's the green car? _*It's between*_ the taxi and the bus.

1. Where's the taxi? _____ the green car.

2. Where's the bus? _____ the green car.

3. Where's Mr. Bascomb? _____ the corner.

4. Where are the firefighters? _____ the fire truck.

5. Where are the Japanese tourists? _____ Barney's taxi.

6. Where are the children? _____ the snack bar.

7. Where's the snack bar? _____ the street from the drugstore.

8. Where are the bicycles? _____ the movie theater.

9. Where's the pet shop? _____ the snack bar.

10. Where's the cat? _____ the roof.

PRACTICE • *Answer the questions about the picture.*

Is Mr. Bascomb crossing the street?
No, he isn't. He's standing at the corner.

Is he looking at the fire truck?
Yes, he is.

1. Is Mr. Bascomb wearing glasses?
2. Is he wearing a hat?
3. Is Barney driving his taxi?
4. Does he have three passengers?
5. Are they Italian?
6. Are the children eating hot dogs?
7. Is the old woman closing the window?
8. Are the dogs chasing the police officer?
9. Are the bicycles in front of the movie theater?
10. Is the drugstore next to the snack bar?

PAIR WORK • *Ask and answer questions.*

A: Where's the cat?
B: **It's on the roof.**

1. Where's Mr. Bascomb?
2. What's he looking at?
3. What's Barney doing?
4. What are his passengers doing?
5. Where's the policeman standing?
6. What are the dogs chasing?

7. What are the children eating?
8. What are they looking at?
9. What's the old woman doing?
10. Is the young woman leaving the drugstore or the movie theater?

CONVERSATION

 Listen and practice.

PETER: Do you like jazz?

MARIA: Yes, very much.

PETER: There's a good concert tonight. Are you free?

MARIA: Sure. Let's go.
OR No, I'm sorry. I'm busy tonight.

PAIR WORK • *Have similar conversations.*

1. basketball
   game/this weekend

2. rock and roll
   concert/Saturday night

3. baseball
   game/tomorrow afternoon

4. classical music
   concert/next week

5. boxing
   fight/Friday night

6. jazz
   concert/tonight

7. football
   game/this Sunday

8. country music
   concert/tomorrow

9. soccer
   game/next Saturday

WRITTEN EXERCISE • *Make a negative sentence for each picture using the verb* **to like.**

1. Peter *doesn't like mayonnaise*.

2. Barbara and Tino *don't like flies*.

3. Mrs. Golo _____.

4. The students _____.

5. Jack _____.

6. Anne _____.

7. The Bascombs _____.

8. Dr. Pasto _____.

CONVERSATION

 Listen and practice.

STOREKEEPER: Can I help you, ma'am?

MABEL BROWN: Yes. I'm looking for some bananas.

STOREKEEPER: I'm sorry. There aren't any bananas left.

MABEL BROWN: Oh, that's too bad!

PAIR WORK • *Have similar conversations.*

A: Can I help you, _____?

B: Yes, I'm looking for some _____.

A: You're lucky. We have some nice

_____ today.

OR I'm sorry. There aren't any

_____ left.

B: Oh, that's wonderful!

OR Oh, that's too bad!

1. apples
2. bananas
3. pears
4. peaches
5. pineapples
6. cherries
7. oranges
8. grapes
9. lemons

WRITTEN EXERCISE • *Write a list of things you need to buy at the market.*

PAIR WORK • *Ask and answer questions using the verb* **to need.**

1. Peter

> A: **What does Peter need?**
> B: **He needs some gas.**

2. Joe and Eddie

> A: **What do Joe and Eddie need?**
> B: **They need a car.**

3.　　　Monty

4.　　　Joe and Eddie

5.　　　Gloria

6.　Betty and Bruno

7.　Mr. Workman

8.　these people

9.　　　Suzi

10.　Joe and Eddie

11.　　　you

Listen and practice.

ROLE PLAY • *Student A plays a tourist, Student B plays a concierge, and Student C plays a bellboy. Act out a scene like the one above. Choose any city.*

CLASS ACTIVITY • *Talk about the picture. What's happening?*

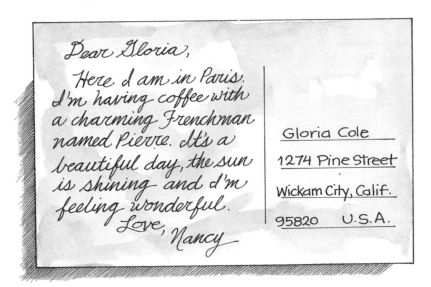

READING

Dear Gloria,

Here I am in Paris. I'm having coffee with a charming Frenchman named Pierre. It's a beautiful day, the sun is shining and I'm feeling wonderful.

Love,
Nancy

Gloria Cole
1274 Pine Street
Wickam City, Calif.
95820   U.S.A.

Answer the questions about the postcard.

1. What city is Nancy in?
2. Who is she having coffee with?
3. What is Pierre like?

4. Why is Nancy feeling so good?
5. Who is Nancy writing to?
6. What is Gloria's address?

PAIR WORK • *Work with a partner and write a similar postcard to a friend.*

• *Ask and answer questions about the pictures.*

1. A: **What is the salesman showing Gloria?**
   B: **He's showing her some tennis shoes.**

2. A: **What is Mable serving her guests?**
   B: **She's serving them some cake.**

3. A: **What is Linda giving Fenwick?**
   B: **She's giving him a bone.**

4. What is Albert bringing Linda?

5. What is Mrs. Mango buying her son?

6. What is Dr. Pasto showing his friends?

7. What is Fenwick bringing Sam?

8. What is Mabel serving her guests?

9. What is Mr. Lassiter buying his daughter?

10. What is Mrs. Golo showing her students?

11. What is Marty giving Mrs. Golo?

12. What is Anne bringing Mr. Bascomb?

Listen and practice.

 PRACTICE 1 • *Here are the contents of Mrs. Golo's handbag. Listen and repeat.*

1. candy   2. money   3. keys   4. pencil   5. address book

6. pen   7. stamps   8. comb   9. brush   10. mirror

PRACTICE 2 • *Close your book. Name three things Mrs. Golo has in her handbag.*

PAIR WORK • *Ask about the contents of your partner's handbag, wallet, or pocket.*

A: **What do you have in your pocket?**
B: **I have my keys, a comb, and some change.**
   OR **I don't have anything.**

change

FREE RESPONSE

1. What are you wearing today? What are the students in your class wearing?
2. Are you a good talker? What do you talk about with your friends?
3. Do you have a camera? What kind is it?
4. Are you a music lover? Do you like rock music? jazz?
5. What is your favorite song? Who is your favorite singer?
6. Do you have a big family? How many brothers and sisters do you have?
7. Do you like American food? How is the food in your country?
8. Is there a market near your house? What street is it on? Is it open now?
9. What do you have in your refrigerator? Is there any ice cream?

1. This is Mr. Poole.

   _____ is a teacher.
   a. Him   c. He
   b. It   d. She

2. _____ book is interesting.
   a. These   c. Those
   b. There   d. This

3. _____ flowers are beautiful.
   a. Those   c. That
   b. There   d. This

4. The table is _____ the kitchen.
   a. on   c. to
   b. at   d. in

5. The umbrella is _____ the floor.
   a. at   c. in
   b. on   d. to

6. Nancy is _____ the airport.
   a. to   c. at
   b. on   d. with

7. Tino _____ thirsty.
   a. is   c. have
   b. has   d. are

8. Are _____ pretty girls?
   a. she   c. them
   b. they   d. her

9. The flowers _____ in the vase.
   a. are   c. be
   b. is   d. have

10. Tino isn't short.

    He's _____.
    a. poor   c. sad
    b. happy   d. tall

11. Those books aren't cheap.

    They're _____.
    a. old   c. small
    b. expensive   d. rich

12. They _____ the bank.
    a. are going   c. are going to
    b. is going   d. going to

13. _____ is that? It's a coffee pot.
    a. Who   c. Where
    b. How   d. What

14. _____ He's at the garage.
    a. Where is he?
    b. What is he?
    c. Who is he?
    d. How is he?

15. _____ They're fine, thank you.
    a. Who are they?
    b. What are they?
    c. How are they?
    d. Where are they?

16. _____ is she going? To the market.
    a. What   c. Who
    b. Where   d. How

17. _____ is he? He's Dr. Pasto.
    a. Where   c. How
    b. What   d. Who

18. Wait _____ Anne.
    a. for   c. to
    b. at   d. from

19. Who is she looking _____?
    a. on   c. to
    b. at   d. from

20. He's listening _____ the radio.
    a. at   c. of
    b. in   d. to

21. Talk _____ them.
    a. to   c. on
    b. at   d. of

22. Put these glasses _____ the table.
    a. to   c. on
    b. in   d. at

23. They don't have _____ books.
    a. there   c. theirs
    b. their   d. them

24. This magazine is _____.
    a. to her   c. hers
    b. her   d. of her

25. That desk is _____.
    a. mine   c. me
    b. my   d. to me

26. Whose apartment is that?

    It's _____.
    a. to him   c. his
    b. Mr. Jones d. him

27. Give the flowers _____.
    a. them   c. to they
    b. their   d. to them

28. That man is hungry.

    Give _____ some food.
    a. he   c. his
    b. her   d. him

29. Mrs. Jones is in Italy.

    Write _____ a letter.
    a. to her   c. hers
    b. her   d. him

30. Do they have a car?

    No, they _____.
    a. don't   c. aren't
    b. doesn't   d. have

31. _____ an apple in the kitchen.
    a. It has   c. It's
    b. There are d. There's

32. Where are the cups?

    _____ on the shelf.
    a. They're   c. There is
    b. There are d. Their

33. What are those?

    _____ dictionaries.
    a. There are c. They're
    b. There's some d. It's a

34. _____ milk in the bottle.
    a. There's some c. It's a
    b. There's a d. There are

35. _____ letters on the desk.
    a. There's   c. Their
    b. There are d. They're

36. What time is it? _____
    a. It's hot.
    b. It's ten dollars.
    c. It's two o'clock.
    d. It's six years old.

37. How old is that watch? _____
    a. It's one o'clock.
    b. It's fifty dollars.
    c. It's expensive.
    d. It's six years old.

38. How much is that computer? _____
    a. It's in the office.
    b. It's five hundred dollars.
    c. It's six years old.
    d. It's very good.

39. Jimmy _____ ice cream.
    a. have   c. likes
    b. like   d. want

40. She's thirsty.

    She _____ a glass of water.
    a. wants   c. have
    b. want   d. likes

Preview

Teacher, see p. x.

GRAMMAR
Can
Simple past
Future with "going to"

FUNCTIONS
Expressing ability/inability
Describing past actions
Expressing intention

Listen and read.

Barney **can** swim, but he **can't** ski.

Jenny and Marty **can** play checkers, but they **can't** play chess.

PAIR WORK 1 • *Ask and answer questions about the pictures.*

1. Bonita/sing?   2. Gladys/sing?   3. Ed/play the guitar? 4. Anne/play the guitar?

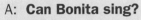
A: **Can Bonita sing?**
B: **Yes, she can.**

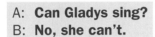
A: **Can Gladys sing?**
B: **No, she can't.**

5. Nancy/speak French? 6. Fred/speak French?   7. Johnnie/swim?   8. Dr. Pasto/swim?

9. Gloria/cook?   10. Ula Hackey/cook?   11. Nick/repair cars?   12. Mr. Bascomb/ repair cars?

PAIR WORK 2 • *Ask your partner the same questions.*

A: **Can you sing?**
B: **Yes, I can.** OR **No, I can't.**

Listen and read.

Yesterday Carlos **got up** at 7 o'clock.

He **took** a shower and **got** dressed.

Then he **had** . breakfast.

At 8:30 he **left** the house and **went** to work.

PICTURE PRACTICE • *Answer the questions about Carlos.*

1. When did Carlos get up yesterday?
2. What did he do after he got up?
3. What did he do then?

4. What did Carlos have for breakfast?
5. When did he leave the house?
6. Where did he go?

PAIR WORK I • *Ask and answer the same questions about Suzi.*

A: **When did Suzi get up yesterday?**
B: **She got up at 6:30.**

 PRACTICE • *Listen and practice.*

Did Suzi get up at 6:30?
Yes, she did.

Did she take a bath?
Yes, she did.

Did she have French fries for breakfast?
No, she didn't. (She had coffee and eggs.)

Did she leave the house at 8:30?
No, she didn't. (She left at 8 o'clock.)

PAIR WORK 2 • *Ask and answer questions about Carlos.*

1. Did Carlos get up at 7 o'clock?
2. Did he take a bath?

3. Did Carlos have orange juice and cereal?
4. Did he leave the house at 9 o'clock?

FREE RESPONSE • *Answer the teacher; then ask your partner these questions.*

1. When did you get up this morning?
2. Did you take a bath or a shower?
3. Did you have a big breakfast?

4. What did you have for breakfast?
5. When did you leave the house?
6. Did you go to the market?

Listen and read.

Yesterday Suzi **went** to the market and **bought** some apples.

Last night Peter and Maria **went** to the Rex Theater and **saw** a movie.

Yesterday afternoon Linda **went** to the library and **studied.**

This morning Barbara and Tino **went** to the park and **played** tennis.

Last night Mr. and Mrs. Golo **stayed** home and **watched** TV.

Last Saturday Johnnie **stayed** home and **read** a book.

SIMPLE PAST Regular Verbs	
play – played	walk – walked
stay – stayed	watch – watched
talk – talked	work – worked

Regular verbs end in -ed.

SIMPLE PAST Irregular Verbs	
go – went	have – had
buy – bought	read – read
do – did	see – saw

For a list of irregular verbs, see the appendix.

PAIR WORK • *Ask and answer questions. Use past time expressions like **yesterday, yesterday afternoon, last night, this morning, last Saturday.***

A: **What did you do last night?**
B: **I went to the Rex Theater and saw a movie. What about you?**
A: **I stayed home and read a book.**
   OR **I didn't do anything.**

Listen and practice.

Barbara and Tino are going to play tennis. Linda is going to see the Beach Bums.

PAIR WORK 1 • *Ask and answer questions about the pictures using **going to**.*

1. A: **What is Anne going to do?**
   B: **She's going to brush her teeth.**

2. A: **What are Carlos and Luisa going to do?**
   B: **They're going to eat dinner.**

1. Anne

2. Carlos and Luisa

3. Nancy

4. the boys

5. Barney

6. Peter and Maria

7. Suzi

8. Otis and Gloria

9. Dr. Pasto

PAIR WORK 2 • *Ask and answer three questions. Use **going to** with future time expressions such as **tonight, tomorrow, Friday night, this weekend,** and so on.*

A: **What are you going to do after class?**
B: **I'm going to study at the library.** OR **I'm going to see my friends.**

Appendix

IRREGULAR VERBS

INFINITIVE	SIMPLE PAST	INFINITIVE	SIMPLE PAST	INFINITIVE	SIMPLE PAST
be	was/were	give	gave	sing	sang
bring	brought	go	went	sit	sat
buy	bought	have	had	speak	spoke
come	came	hold	held	stand	stood
cut	cut	know	knew	swim	swam
do	did	leave	left	take	took
drink	drank	lose	lost	teach	taught
drive	drove	make	made	tell	told
eat	ate	meet	met	think	thought
feed	fed	put	put	understand	understood
find	found	read	read	wear	wore
fly	flew	ride	rode	win	won
forget	forgot	see	saw	write	wrote
get	got	shine	shone		

TAPESCRIPT FOR PAGE 81

It's Sunday afternoon. There are a lot of people at the corner of Sunset and Main. Jenny and Marty are sitting in a tree. They're waving to Barbara and Tino, who are riding their bicycles. Peter and Maria are walking on the sidewalk. They're smiling and holding hands. Johnnie is standing next to the tree. He's eating an apple. Otis and Gloria are having a conversation. They're talking about the new movie at the Plaza Theater. Suzi is buying a ticket for the movie. It's a nice day and everyone is having a good time.

CHAPTER ONE

ey

name	bookcase
vase	airplane
table	newspaper
station	

ae

cat	apple
hat	taxi
that	rabbit
glass	mechanic

airplane

CHAPTER TWO

ay

time	pilot
like	library
fine	bicycle
nice	behind

i

this	city
big	window
rich	single
thin	chicken

CHAPTER THREE

s

hats	pilots	cups
coats	students	pots
books	trucks	clocks
lamps	streets	desks

The books and lamps are on the desk.
Give Otis the rabbits and cats.

z

apples	boys	pens
pears	girls	letters
flowers	tables	cards
candles	chairs	bottles

Talk to those boys and girls.
Read those letters and magazines.

iz

vases	buses	watches
glasses	nurses	messages
dishes	matches	houses
oranges	dresses	addresses

The sandwiches and oranges are for the nurses.
Give them the glasses and dishes, too.

nurses

Those cars, buses, and trucks are new.
Please wash these cups, bottles, and dishes.
The pilots are with the doctors and nurses.

CHAPTER FIVE

i

give	dish	big
him	with	kiss
this	it	sit
little	rich	kitchen

Give Nick this picture.
His little sister is in the kitchen.

iy

we	beach	meet
tea	cheap	please
street	eat	read
clean	leave	green

Please meet the teacher at the museum.
The streets are clean and the tea is green.

Jimmy is cleaning the windows.
He isn't reading his magazine.

CHAPTER SIX

ae

happy	class	ask
sad	handbag	man
glad	stand	candle
bad	lamp	camera

Nancy has a black hat.
The happy dancer is laughing at the fat cat.

e

red	telephone	ready
desk	expensive	envelope
bed	dress	television
pen	letter	message

The red dress is very expensive.
Fred's letter is in the envelope.

Ellen has a telegram in her handbag.
The black hat is next to the red lamp.

CHAPTER SEVEN

ay

time	buy	mine
write	pipe	by
shine	white	slice
bicycle	pilot	like

Simon's pipe is by the typewriter.
The white bicycle is behind the library.

ey

cake	vase	make
paper	bookcase	take
airplane	favorite	eight
plate	chase	game

Take the vase and the plates to Miss Paine.
Mabel is making a cake today.

I'm waiting for an airplane pilot.
Jane likes cake and ice cream.

VOCABULARY

The vocabulary lists include all of the words that appear chapter-by-chapter in *Exploring English*. Nouns are given in the singular only. With the exception of Chapter One, verbs are given in the infinitive form. To find the simple past of irregular verbs, see page 141.

Parts of speech have been omitted except for words that can be used as more than one part of speech. These abbreviations are used:
adj. = adjective; adv. = adverb; n. = noun; prep. = preposition; v. = verb.

CHAPTER I

a	cat	hospital	pear	under
airport	chair	how	pilot	
am	chicken		police officer	vase
an	clock	I	post office	
and	coat	in front of		watch (n.)
apple		is	rabbit	what
are	doctor	it		where
artist	dog		secretary	who
at		library	she	
	egg		singer	yes
ball	envelope	mechanic		you
bank		movie star	table	your
banker	flower	museum	taxi driver	
behind		my	teacher	
bird	garage		that	
book	gas station	name	the	
bookcase	glass	newspaper	these	
bottle	good	next to	they	
bus		no	this	
businessman	hat	not	those	
bus stop	he		to	
	hello		too	
car	her	office	tree	
card	his	on	truck	
		orange		

Expressions

Hello. What's your name?
My name's Maria.
Nice to meet you.

Hi.
Good-bye.
See you later.

Good morning. How are you?
I'm fine. And you?
Fine, thank you.

Where's Nick?
He's at the garage.
What's his job?
He's a mechanic.

CHAPTER 2

airplane	clean (adj.)	friend	magazine	Russian	two
American	cold	from	man		
	color		married	sad	ugly
bad	country	German	meeting	school	umbrella
ballet	cowboy	girl	Mexican	shirt	university
beautiful		good	modern	shoe	
bicycle	dancer	guitar		short	waiter
big	desk		nationality	singer	wastebasket
blond	dictionary	handsome	new	single	we
blouse	dirty	happy		small	window
boy	dress (n.)	history	old	Spanish	with
Brazilian		home	one	student	woman
building	English	hot		stupid	work
business	expensive	hungry	pants		
by	eye		poor	tall	young
		intelligent	postcard	teacher	
capital	fat	Italian	pot	thin	
cheap	favorite		pretty	thirsty	
city	floor	letter		time	
classroom	French	living room	rich	tourist	

Expressions

What time is it?	Where are you from?	How much is it?	Excuse me.	at home
It's five o'clock.	What's it like?	It's fifty dollars.	Thank you.	at work
				at school

Colors

red	green	gray
yellow	orange	black
blue	brown	white

Opposites

hot/cold	big/small	good/bad	beautiful/ugly
fat/thin	old/young	happy/sad	intelligent/stupid
short/tall	old/new	rich/poor	expensive/cheap

Numbers 1–20

1 one	6 six	11 eleven	16 sixteen
2 two	7 seven	12 twelve	17 seventeen
3 three	8 eight	13 thirteen	18 eighteen
4 four	9 nine	14 fourteen	19 nineteen
5 five	10 ten	15 fifteen	20 twenty

CHAPTER 3

across	dance (v.)	give	light (v.)	parking lot	take
address	dangerous	go	listen	past	talk
afternoon	day	gun	little	price	telephone
all	desk		look (v.)	put	them
answer	department store	here			there
ask	dinner	him	ma'am	question	tonight
	dish	hotel	match (n.)		touch
barber shop	do	house	message	read	
bed	dollar	housewife	midnight	really	us
blackboard	door		minute	repeat	
book store	dresser	immediately	money	right	wait (v.)
bring	drugstore	important	morning	room	wall
		incredible	much		wash
call	each			sandwich	why
cafe	eat	kitchen	near	shelf	worry
candle	emergency		noon	sir	write
church	evening	lamp	now	sit down	
class		large		sofa	year
close (v.)	father	laugh	of	stand up	
come	fire	leave	open	street	
couch	fire department	lesson	outside	supermarket	
cup		letter			

Expressions

Please.	Here you are.	Don't worry.	My house is on fire.	all right
Let's talk.	Have a nice day.	Dinner's ready.	It's hot in here.	right away

He's a big man.
So are you.

CHAPTER 4

afraid	dental floss	hamburger	mouth	snake	use
animal	do	horse	mouthwash	soda	
apple pie	doughnut	hot dog	move (v.)	spider	waiter
aspirin					
	forget	ice cream	orange juice	teeth	
bill	front desk			think	
	fruit	lion	pain	ticket	
cheese					
coffee	get up	more	rat		

Expressions

What does he do?	OK, that's it.	That's right.	Oh, my!	one way
He's a singer.	Are you all right?	Here we are.	I'm busy.	round trip
Anything else?	Don't be afraid.	Thank you.	Hurry up.	
I'm not sure.	You're in good hands.	Not at all.	Bye.	

CHAPTER 5

about	computer	goodbye	menu	prepare	Sunday
	cook (v.)	grass	milk		
basketball	counter		mirror	radio	tea
bath	cut (v.)	hair	Monday	repair (v.)	television
bathroom		help	mother	rest (v.)	today
beach	darts	hold (v.)		restaurant	
beige	draw	homework	night	ride (v.)	walk (v.)
breakfast	drink (v.)	husband	nightgown		water
brother			nothing	say	wave (v.)
brush (v.)	family	kiss		shine (v.)	wear
buy	floor		paint (v.)	shower	week
	football	lemonade	pajamas	sidewalk	wife
cashier	for	long	park	sister	
cigar		lunch	pay (v.)	smile (v.)	
clean (v.)	game		picture	snack bar	
coffeeshop	get	make	play (v.)	sun	

Expressions
What a sweet life!

CHAPTER 6

also	cute	important	name (v.)	president	their
apartment		interesting	neighbor		thing
average	famous			record player	television
	friendly	job	our	refrigerator	
boyfriend				roof	vegetable
brush (.n)	garden	key	paper		
but	girlfriend	kind	party	save	wallet
	glasses		pen	smile (n.)	whose
camera		long	pencil	son	wonderful
candy	handbag		phone	stamp	
change	have	mirror	piano		
classic	height	money	piece	taxi	
comb	homework		pocket		

Expressions

Good to see you!   Are you having a good time?   What's it like?
What a great car.   I'm too busy.   It's wonderful?

Oh, really?   That's OK.   Wow!
That's good.   Right now.   Boy!

CHAPTER 7

any	carrot	fried	notebook	rice	trash
around	cereal	front yard		roast beef	typewriter
athlete	chase		olive	rock music	
	cherry	ham	onion	rose	use
bag	chocolate	hour	opera		
balcony	classical			sidewalk	vegetable
banana	coffee pot	jar	page	sink (n.)	visitor
baseball	collection		people	slice (n.)	
bathtub	cookie	ketchup	pepper	some	waitress
bedroom	corn	knife	photograph	soup	want
belong	corn flakes		picnic	spaghetti	wash basin
boot	cucumber	lettuce	piece	sport	watch (v.)
bowl		life	pig	statue	which
box	every	like (v.)	pitcher	step (n.)	wide
bread	expert		pizza	stove	wine
bunch		map	plant (v.)	string bean	wire
butter	fence	mayonnaise	plate		
butterfly	fireplace	mine	popular	tea	yard
	fish	moment	potato	team	
cafe	flag	month	professor	theater	
cake	flies (n.)	mushroom		toilet	
calendar	food	music	radish	tomato	
can (n.)	French fries	mustard	raise (n.)	traditional	

CHAPTER 8

actor	comb	face	July	painting	story
art	comedy	feel (v.)		passenger	strange
August	composition	firefighter	key	personality	strong
author	concert	first		pet shop	
	country western	Frenchman	lemon	pineapple	tennis shoes
bags	cross (v.)		love (v.)	program	true
band		gas	lover	public	
biography	December	grape			unusual
birthday	different	guest	many	sale	
bone	disco		me	science fiction	vacation
boxing	drama	historical	musical	serve (v.)	vegetarian
	drive (v.)		mystery	shape	
candy		idea		show (v.)	western
cartoon	enjoy	include	news	soccer	when
certain	exhibition			song	
change (n.)	expression	Japanese	ordinary	star	
charming		jazz	original	stay (v.)	

Expressions

Let's go.	Can I help you?	Let's see.	very much	Are you free?
Good idea.	You're welcome.	It's for sale.	at the moment	No, I'm busy.